ARCHIPENKO:
DRAWINGS, RELIEFS, AND CONSTRUCTIONS

EXHIBITION CURATOR: JOAN MARTER

RESEARCH ASSOCIATE: NICHOLAS J. CAPASSO

THIS EXHIBITION HAS BEEN ORGANIZED
WITH FUNDS FROM THE
EDITH C. BLUM FOUNDATION

ORGANIZED AND PUBLISHED BY THE
EDITH C. BLUM ART INSTITUTE
BARD COLLEGE CENTER
ANNANDALE-ON-HUDSON, NY

ACKNOWLEDGEMENTS

There is no greater privilege for a director of a college art institute than to present the work of a universally acclaimed artist, to organize this exhibition under the guidance of a distinguished scholar, and to benefit throughout the months of preparation from advice offered by the two individuals who are most intimately acquainted with the artist's career—his widow and his dealer.

The exhibition and the catalog will serve to acknowledge the genius of the artist himself. Alexander Archipenko's contribution to 20th century art has never been more apparent than it is within the context of work being produced today. His daring experiments with color, form, and material, and his lifelong willingness to associate convention with the constraints of dogma led him to establish revolutionary new precedents for generations of younger artists to explore.

Professor Joan Marter has brought to this project not only a stellar set of qualifications, but a focus that enabled her to organize a monumental amount of material, and to extract from it a fresh new point of view. Her efforts have assured that this exhibition and its catalogue will make a lasting contribution to the literature relating to sculpture in the 20th century. She was assisted in her efforts by Priscilla Schwarz, Karl Sandin, and Donna Gustafson who, in sharing the responsibilities, also deserve to share the credits.

Robert Rosenblum contributed a fascinating statement revealing the evolution of his personal relationship to Archipenko's work. Because of Professor Rosenblum's stature within the academic community, any personal statement must be viewed as having significance and interest to all readers. He has become a spokesman for the art community—his personal observations contain general truths. The introduction that he wrote establishes the rationale for this entire project.

Nicholas J. Capasso conducted much of the research and contributed both the entries on the individual works of art and the extensive bibliography. He has furnished resource material that will provide scholars and the general audience with access to a wealth of information that would otherwise have been extremely difficult to attain.

Frances Gray and Virginia Zabriskie have cooperated with every phase of this project—from the initial inception to its culmination. Without their guidance and their participation this project would not have been possible. Both have a clear and precise understanding of the historic significance of Archipenko's career. Their dedication to conveying this to art audiences has guaranteed the scholarly merits of this project as well as the beauty of the presentation.

The Edith C. Blum Foundation has recognized the importance of this project by funding both the exhibition and the catalog. This is the third exhibition that this foundation has supported. Its commitment to the principles by which the Blum Art Institute operates have thereby been established—to promote the advancement of scholarship in art history. Without the generous support of the foundation, this institute could not fulfill its potential nor serve its audience.

The Bard College staff has participated in each task essential to mounting a show of this calibre. Each has contributed in some vital way, so that the final product is the expression of the most desirable kind of group effort. I'd like to extend a special expression of gratitude to the members of this team: Iris Kufert, assistant to the director; Mirko Gabler, preparator; Lucy Ferriss, director of publications; Tina Green, director of public relations; Ann Gabler, program development associate; Judy Samoff, director of grants; Dick Griffiths, director of physical plant; Ed Martin, director of security; Don Bennett, dining services manager.

Every project at the Blum Institute requires, simultaneously, the vigilance and guidance of two special members of the administration: Dimitri Papadimitriou, executive vice president, and Leon Botstein, president, and of Wilbur Friedman, chairman of the Board of Overseers. Appreciation for their loyal support is recognized with absolute sincerity.

It is a privilege to have worked with each individual mentioned in the preceding paragraphs. It is my hope that the visitors to this exhibition and the readers of this catalogue will share in my recognition of their efforts.

Linda Weintraub
Director of the Institute

Lenders to the exhibition:

Frances Archipenko Gray

Zabriskie Gallery

Yale University Art Gallery

Gerald Peters Gallery

TABLE OF CONTENTS AND LIST OF PLATES

Archipenko

A METAPHYSICAL CUBIST

"The art of the young Russian, Archipenko, who works in Paris, presses toward a new thing as yet unseen . . . Aside from a couple of very agitated and confusing figures, sculpture has hitherto been only a melody. The works of Archipenko are harmony—its first chords."

With characteristic insight, Guillaume Apollinaire greeted Archipenko's first one-person exhibition in 1912 with this statement. He perceived that both Neo-Classicism and Impressionism, the two prevailing sculptural modes, were being suddenly undermined by this artist who was presenting revolutionary and unprecedented alternatives.

Archipenko devoted his long and productive career to exploring the possibilities for creative invention that were contained in these early experiments. But what is even more significant, he contributed to the sculptural vocabulary new options that have challenged subsequent generations of sculptors. To list the innovations that have been credited to Archipenko is to define many of the unique elements of 20th century sculpture. And yet, it is perhaps too flippant to state that Archipenko created the sculptural vocabulary of modern art. It is even mistaken to attribute to him, as many scholars have done, the transformation of cubist painting into three-dimensional form.

Archipenko was a participant in the pageant of experimentation in Paris. He arrived there in 1907 from his native Kiev. He came formed by the lessons he had learned as a student in the Ukraine and in Moscow and impressed by the examples of art he had observed there. As a result, the French experience had to be adjusted to suit these predispositions. Indeed, he did not seem to relate as naturally to the form and content of Cubism as to the revolutionary spirit and the zeal which characterized the movement.

One wonders if, had Archipenko lived in a period less responsive to and respectful of change, the honored list of innovations associated with his name would have been any less extensive. For Archipenko, invention seemed to be a natural product of thought, not a dramatic act of defiance. He believed that those who pursued the known course were subject to the constraints of dogma—an intolerable interference with artistic freedom. One reason why it is inappropriate to relate Archipenko too closely with Cubism is because he felt that all convention interfered with creative exploration, whether it was the convention of academic art or the conventions of the avant garde.

The two periods of greatest invention for Archipenko were the first decade of his working life, which coincided with the Cubist experiment, and the last, which is the focus of the current exhibition. The intervening years were spent in an effort to rise to the challenge he had imposed upon himself in those early years—to explore their full significance and to evolve a formal system of thought based upon their implications. These inventions encompassed every element of the art-making process: all materials, all methods, all possibilities of texture, form, color, light, space, reflection, and transparency. Each of these elements will be discussed in the following pages, and their relationship to Cubism will be suggested. The reader is urged to be mindful of the fact that even when formal aspects of Archipenko's work seem to coincide with elements of the Cubist style invented by Picasso and Braque, the origins and intentions of these aspects often differ.

FORM

Archipenko questioned the concept of form that for hundreds of years had come to be the exclusive concern of sculptors: Was form limited to the manipulation of solid matter? Archipenko coaxed into the sculptor's vocabulary two heretical options. One was the form-giving capacity of the void; the other was concavity. Both brought Archipenko's work into conformity with the Cubist's tendency to reject the concept of form as being solid, enduring, palpable, and essentially opposed to the empty and formless space that surrounded it. Instead, form and space were represented as having shared characteristics. They were contingent aspects of physical reality.

In a similar manner, concave shapes define a form that is absent. The space that fills the hollow acquires definition and character and functions actively as an element of the sculpture. Concavity summons the awareness of what is not present, and therefore implies its opposite.

Both the void and concavity were utilized by Archipenko to expand the viewer's consciousness—because they are intangible, they served to propel the viewer into an awareness of metaphysical manners of thought. Archipenko, a son of Russian parents, attempted to utilize this expansion by urging it into a spiritual realm. The Cubist painters, on the other hand, seemed intent on expanding the viewer's awareness of the nature of the physical environment. They scrutinized the structure of matter and recorded the known, as opposed to the perceived environment. But their concerns rarely extended into the psychological and metaphysical realms.

SHAPE

Archipenko denied indebtedness to Picasso and Cubism to explain his frequent use of such elementary shapes as the cylinder and the cone. He insisted that he was more keenly affected by Assyrian, Egyptian, Hindu, early Byzantine, Gothic, and archaic Greek art than by that of the Cubists. Use of these basic geometric forms emerged naturally out of the circumstances imposed by the new materials out of which he had begun to construct his art. Sheet metal can only be bent in two ways; it either produces a cone or a cylinder. This geometrization was an inevitability caused by material necessity. The medium determined the parameters of shape.

Indeed, when Archipenko's work in other materials is examined, it becomes apparent that his natural predilection was to explore fluent lines and swelling curves. This fact may explain why he was obsessed with the female form throughout his long career. His was a mannerist style.

Nonetheless, the reduction of subject in his metal work into its formal elements is associable with Cubism. In both cases this simplification allowed one shape to serve, simultaneously, as an aspect of two or more separate objects. A single unit could function as an arm, a neck, or a musical instrument, background intermingled with foreground, and the work became capable of being infinitely reinterpreted. Although each element can never be known with certainty, this lack is compensated by the fact that it expands to contain all possibilities.

The tendency to divide an object into elements so that it becomes nonspecific allows the art object to function, in Archipenko's words, "as symbol, association and relativity." Forms become so broadly applicable that they are capable of evoking "visions of our ancestral past," as well as allowing us to gain access to "the nebulous future." Materiality, thereby, transcends itself in Archipenko's sculpture.

In contrast, materiality in Cubist painting dissolves into an array of molecules occupying indefinable spatial currents. It sheds its substance but seems never to acquire Archipenko's spiritual resonance.

COLOR

In Archipenko's pursuit of ways to invest "dead matter" with "a living soul" he continually incorporated new and untraditional elements in his work. One such element was color, which had been banished from sculpture for several centuries. The reintroduction of color provided the artist with an extraordinary expansion of creative options. Essentially, it afforded the means of incorporating into sculpture all of the techniques of production and manners of viewing that had been the exclusive domain of painting.

Archipenko employed color, applied in paint to three-dimensional forms, to produce the illusionistic effects conventionally reserved for painting. For instance, paint was capable of visually dissolving form, thereby dematerializing the surface on which it was placed. At the same time, paint could suggest boundaries that did not actually exist, producing the illusion of forms existing in physical reality. It could undermine actual spatial locations by incorporating the implied distances created out of tone and value, and it could create the illusion of distance which competed with the actual placement of forms within the relief.

These effects related, once again, to the Cubist painters whose images deliberately resisted visual clarity. Definition and measure were thought to be deceptive of the actual workings of the physical universe. The painted image portrayed the reality of a relativistic world, one in which nothing could be known with certainty.

Archipenko's frank acceptance of the decorative value of color, however, differentiated him from the Cubists who tended to limit the palette to monochromatic effects. They not only neutralized the color of individual objects, they standardized surface textures, so that each element within a Cubist composition, by being stripped of its identifying color and texture, lost its association with a particular object. The Cubist's universe was comprised of homologous units. Its parts were, therefore, interchangeable and the composite effect, ambiguous.

In Cubist paintings, the treatment of form was extended and applied in similar fashion to space. As a result, for Archipenko and for the Cubist painters, the void was presented undifferentiated from the material universe—both were presented as having shape, tone and texture.

MIXED MEDIA

This presents a startling contrast to the second technique employed by Archipenko to incorporate polychromy into sculpture. He broke another respected tradition in Western sculpture by denying its material unity. Paper maché, glass, wood, metal, wire, and lucite were all employed in a single work of art. Because each material was allowed to retain its identifying color and texture, the resulting images broke with the monotone appearance of Cubist painting. Archipenko's works were bold, ebullient, sumptuous, and varied.

Archipenko's intention was to suggest the infinite variety he had observed in life and in nature. He attempted to connect art to the modern environment by mirroring its complexity.

REFLECTION AND TRANSPARENCY

Some of the new materials Archipenko employed were reflective, contributing to the indecipherable merging of objects with other objects, and between objects and their environment. This quality was further enhanced through the introduction of transparent materials. Transparency, like reflection, reduces the materiality of the work of art; it eradicates boundaries and dissolves silhouettes. In both of these instances the effect was comparable to the regularized vocabulary of forms which unified the Cubist surface.

MOTION

These tendencies culminated in Archipenko's invention of Archipentura—a machine that produced the effect of motion. Motion literally expressed dynamism, a quality Archipenko identified as being an aspect of all things and the essential truth of the universe. Although Cubist painting always appears to be shifting—the images pulsate and cannot be fixed in space—Archipenko literalized movement, and through movement, time and the fourth dimension actually enter the arena of art.

The current exhibition will not only present a series of constructions and reliefs which present masterful examples of each of the innovations outlined in this essay, it will also include a collection of gouaches, prints, and drawings. These two-dimensional works of art provide a fascinating indication of how Archipenko, having explored the possibilities of expanding the sculptural vocabulary to include color, mixed materials, reflection, transparency, and motion, reapplied these lessons to his two-dimensional works. These pieces are equally pioneering. In them Archipenko creates the luminosity, the sense of interior spaces, the feeling of parts being constructed out of independent units, the contrast between tangible and optical realities, and the sense of growth and change which have become hallmarks of Archipenko's style. In freeing himself from preconceived ideas about art, Archipenko also broke the boundaries of expectation that each viewer brings to the art experience. In examining a work of art by Archipenko, the visual sense is expanded so that not only is more seen, but things are perceived more deeply. It is easy to succumb to Archipenko's own edict. His work, he says, is "Dedicated to every mother, to everyone who is in love and suffers from love, to everyone who creates in the arts and in science; to every hero, to everyone who is lost in problems; to everyone who knows and feels Eternity and Infinity."

Linda Weintraub

NOTES ON Archipenko's CLEOPATRA

Nobody could have been more surprised than I when, in 1979, in the midst of my regular gallery rounds, I looked in at the Zabriskie Gallery to check dutifully and, I hoped, quickly an exhibition of late sculpture by Archipenko. My expectations could hardly have been lower. All art-historical catechisms had taught us that Archipenko entered the dramatic story of the making of modern art way back in the heyday of Cubism and Futurism when, for a decade or so, he had been an audacious innovator who could put a hole in the middle of a solid bronze sculpture, who could confound the medium of polychrome painting with that of low relief, who could flout sculptural traditions by adulterating his works with such alien materials as glass or wire. But we had also been taught that if Archipenko himself lived to be a senior citizen, dying in 1964 at the age of 77, the longevity of his art was another matter. Presumably, his artistic energy burned out fast, like that of many of his rebel contemporaries born in the 1880s, and the products of his later decades would inspire nothing but embarrassed yawns, regrets, and averted eyes. This pattern of a meteoric flash and eclipse was a familiar one in our assumptions about many early 20th-century artists who seemed to exist for only a few brilliant years, usually just before, during, or after the First World War, and who then were written off the holy tablets of art history. Sometimes, as in the cases of Boccioni, Marc, and Duchamp-Villon, they actually lost their young lives in the Great War; but in terms of the later history of art, had they gone on living and working, it might have made hardly a difference, or so it seemed in the case of the later reputation of survivors like Severini or Archipenko.

But contrary to such prejudiced expectations, an enormous polychrome relief by Archipenko—some seven feet wide—stopped me in my tracks. By all conventions, everything about it was wrong. It was executed in 1957, at a time when all our attention was supposed to be directed toward Abstract Expressionism, and to the beginnings of Johns and Rauschenberg; it was made from the most synthetic-looking materials, from a sleek woodgrain finish to a still sleeker bakelite surface that conflicted with the organic, rough and ragged textures of most high art of that decade; and it employed a vocabulary of smoothly looping, boomerang shapes which interlocked with jigsaw-puzzle precision and which evoked an industrial manufacture completely antagonistic to the prevailing taste for the handmade and the irregular. And as a final blow, it had the oddest subject, Cleopatra, who we may have thought expired with the Orientalist fantasies of the 19th century, but who here seemed reborn, a weirdly plastic creature who reclined voluptuously on a full-length couch, beside what appeared to be a trapezoidal tray of jewelry, and who contemplated her ancient beauty in a *trompe l'oeil* mirror that startlingly protruded above the upper frame.

From any angle, this imposing relief jarred against every preconception about what was good or bad art; but it nevertheless had the kind of grand-scale, stubborn presence that refused to go away and that could perhaps re-enter the history of art in other, more surprising ways. For one thing, I began to realize that *Cleopatra* intersected the 1950s not through the familiar painting and sculpture of that decade, but through the broader domain of a period style in the decorative arts. In fact, the new post-war design of the 1950s, with its fusion of clean, synthetic materials, glossy surfaces, and the pulsating contours of belated Surrealist biomorphs as frozen by laminated wood, bakelite, or wire tracery, is encapsulated and inventoried here. The ghosts of spindly Olivetti desks, of the 1951 Festival of Britain, of free-form coffee tables, of those French lamps, neon signs, and coat hangers that invaded space with linear mazes of sharp, but ductile rhythms—such visual memories hover over *Cleopatra* and give it the kind of period nostalgia that the later 20th century has been cultivating in an ever-more retrospective view of a century that once seemed only to face the future, but that now looks very much to the past.

It is exactly this kind of rearrangement of historical attitudes and aesthetic preferences that now, in the 1980s, is beginning to make it possible to look freshly, from what might be called a post-Modernist view, at quantities of 20th-century art that had been swept under the carpet by the relentless forward drive of Modernism. Nothing has benefited more from this new refusal to accept the fixed values of the earlier century than the later work of those modern masters whose relevance to the ongoing story of modern art was thought to have stopped abruptly in their youth. Even Picasso's late work, once scorned by the majority of serious Picassophiles, has become, in recent years, the object of new passion and discovery; and this story is repeated in the enthusiasm elicited by the late work of such long-lived masters, once thought artistically short-lived, as Chagall, Picabia, and deChirico. Here, as is often the case in the story of drastic shifts of taste, it is the younger artist who leads the way. The free-floating fantasies of Clemente, for example, make us see the late work of Chagall with newer, more sympathetic eyes; the see-through superpositions of realist drawings on abstract grounds in the work of Polke or Salle give the late Picabia a new lease on life; Warhol's variations on deChirico's own late variations and replications of his early work add new dimensions to the Chinese-box fascination of the reproduction of reproductions; and so it goes with Archipenko's *Cleopatra* too. For surely, this species of plastic temptress, a sex-goddess from an extraterrestrial machine world, rather than being dead and buried with the 1950s, has been resurrected in the work of such younger painters as Jedd Garet, who populates his Neo-Surrealist spaces with a progeny of slickly-contoured, featureless humanoids that might have stemmed from Cleopatra's own loins. As always, new art changes old art; and it would seem that in the 1980s, Archipenko's later work may make many artists and spectators rub their eyes with wonder. For me, at least, *Cleopatra* has already become a roadblocking challenge that reshuffles the past, present, and future of what happened in 20th-century art.

Robert Rosenblum

FIGURE 1
CLEOPATRA, (REPOSE) 1957
Wood, bakelite, polychrome
38×84″
Collection: Frances Archipenko Gray

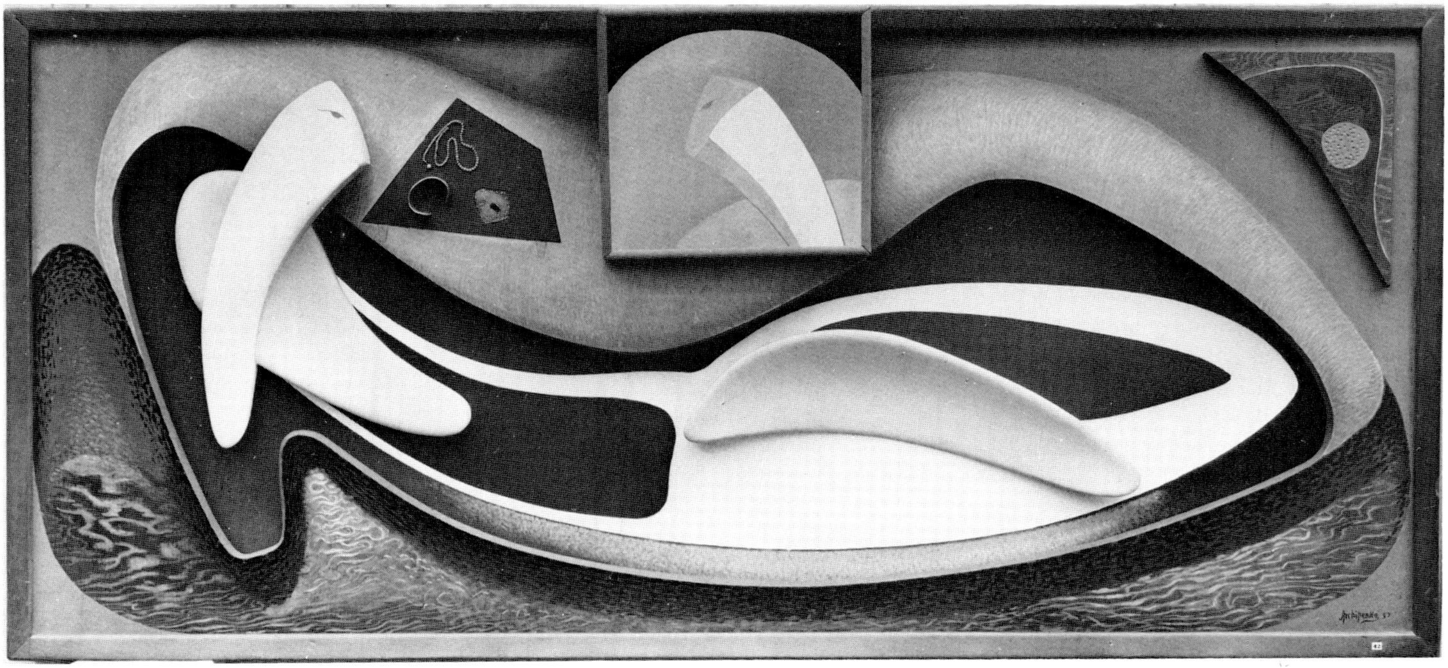

Alexander Archipenko
THEMES AND VARIATIONS

I. ARCHIPENKO IN RETROSPECT

Alexander Archipenko (1887-1964) was one of the great sculptural innovators of the early twentieth century.[1] Plastic discoveries he made during the Cubist period sustained him through five decades of creative activity. In his late years the sculptor again surged forward with fresh inventions that were both the culmination of his lifelong commitment to modernist principles, and fully realized personal visions of great power.

It is the production of his later life, particularly polychrome reliefs and related works on paper, that is the focus of this exhibition. While the majority of these works were exhibited during the artist's lifetime, some examples have not been published previously. In addition, retrospective exhibitions of Archipenko's sculpture have not given special consideration to the multi-media constructions of the 1950s and early 1960s. The 1957 reliefs in polychrome wood and bakelite found a difficult reception when they were first shown. The bravado of expressive line, vivid color, and bold texture of his 1960s gouache and ink figure studies also proved too shocking a contrast to the reductivist abstractions of those years.[2] However, these works are now being presented as examples of Archipenko's late style that can be recognized for their special character within the artist's oeuvre. The last decade of the artist's career has already been acclaimed as a "period of greatest inventiveness"[3] to parallel his first decade of sculptural activity. The late reliefs, sculpto-paintings, related drawings, and prints included in the current exhibition bear out this assessment. Archipenko allowed his creative investigations to come full circle—to form a striking link with his earliest polychrome sculpto-paintings.

If these works are now receiving the recognition that they merit, changes in aesthetic sensibilities are one reason; recent art historical revisionism in the assessment of late works by modern masters is another (Pablo Picasso, Georgio di Chirico, and Francis Picabia have received similar studies). Archipenko's late works also offer new possibilities for the interpretation of his entire artistic production; for this sculptor has often been described as a Cubist, and has been assessed mostly on the basis of the formal innovations of his early years. While Archipenko is justifiably acclaimed for his first multi-media constructions and his fresh explorations of sculptural mass and space, his later years are also rich with achievements of a very personal nature that cannot be defined in terms of a single stylistic idiom.

Archipenko's art transcends purely formal considerations, although the sculptor was deeply sensitive to the properties of color, line, shape, and texture. Late in his life he spoke about the spiritual basis of his art:

> *First of all it should be stated that in spite of the diversity in the character of my works, no intellectual or dogmatic rules lie at the foundation of my art. Fundamentally it is spiritual, and evolved from the universal creative law perceived through experiences. This law compels me to explore the unknown and to invent a way to fix it in new forms. I believe that the whole evolution of art and inventions is based exclusively on the material fixation of the unknown, as a consequence of our attainment of causes in the metaphysical realm.*[4]

There are many cultural sources for Archipenko's creative production. He was a Ukrainian by birth, and remained indebted throughout his career to the spiritual values and visual effects found in the Byzantine culture of his youth. He had a strong affinity for Egyptian, Gothic, and primitive art that co-existed with the influence of modernist styles like Cubism and Futurism. His art was also deeply informed by personal experiences. Born into a Ukrainian family in which the grandfather was an icon-maker and the father was an engineer/inventor, Archipenko appropriated aspects of both these callings for his art. He sought eternal values—the ritualistic art of giving form to the spiritual in the tradition of the creators of icons. Archipenko was also inventive—giving dynamic expression to contemporary life, experimenting with industrial materials and found objects within the aesthetics of modernism.

This sculptor was a man of his time, rejecting the outworn classicism that survived into the twentieth century. While he is known for actively introducing spatial volumes into sculptural compositions, even this fundamental element of his sculpture—his use of space—is associated with the spiritual realm.

Archipenko was born May 30, 1887 in Kiev, Ukraine, Russia. At age thirteen he was injured on his bicycle, and while confined to his bed for many months he copied drawings by Michelangelo. The fact that his grandfather was an artist and his father a professor of engineering at the University of Kiev had major influence on his course of study as a youth. Archipenko took as his model Leonardo da Vinci, who was both artist and inventor. While he enrolled in art school to study painting and sculpture, he never lost sight of the scientific basis for the study of all forms in nature. Hildebrandt attributed Archipenko's interest in experimentation and his "keen sense for the essentially mathematical proportion of things" to his family background.[5]

Archipenko studied at the Academy of Art in Kiev, but he was forced to leave in 1905 after he criticized the conservative academicism of his instructors. The following year the young artist went to Moscow where he participated in some group shows and saw an exhibition of French Impressionists that helped motivate him to go to Paris.[6] After the Ukrainian youth had established himself in Paris in 1909[7], he proceeded to reject the most favored sculptural styles of the period, including the work of Auguste Rodin. Formal instruction at the Ecole des Beaux-Arts lasted only two weeks before he left to learn sculpture by direct study of examples in the Louvre. His lifelong interest in polychromy and anatomical stylizations was manifest at the outset by his preference for Egyptian, archaic Greek, and early Gothic works.

Archipenko's first sculptures, in their stress on solid mass, showed the impact of another source, the art of the ancient Americas. While in Paris he set up a studio in Montparnasse where he was soon producing three-dimensional works with an emphasis on active contours. By 1912 the twenty-five-year-old artist had opened his own art school, and had come under the influence of the Cubists. The collages of Picasso and Braque were important to Archipenko's creation of the first construction in painted materials, *Medrano I* (Juggler) that included glass, metal and wire (Fig. 2).[8] These multi-media constructions, as well as the related sculpto-paintings in painted plaster, were also closely related to the *Technical Manifesto of Futurist Sculpture* published by Umberto Boccioni in 1912.[9]

Other innovations of this period included the opening up of the volumes of the sculpted figure, the reversal of convex and concave elements, as well as the piercing of sculptural mass. All of these Cubist-related abstractions caused controversy when they were first exhibited. Archipenko joined the Section d'Or group in Paris in 1912, and in the same year he began to receive international recognition for his achievements.

Beginning in 1910 Archipenko submitted his sculptures to the Salon des Indépendants, and to the Salon d'Automne from 1911. By 1913 the sculptor was included in the Armory show in New York, the Herbstsalon in Berlin, and the International Post-Impressionist exhibition in Budapest.[10] During the following year the sculptor showed one of his

FIGURE 2

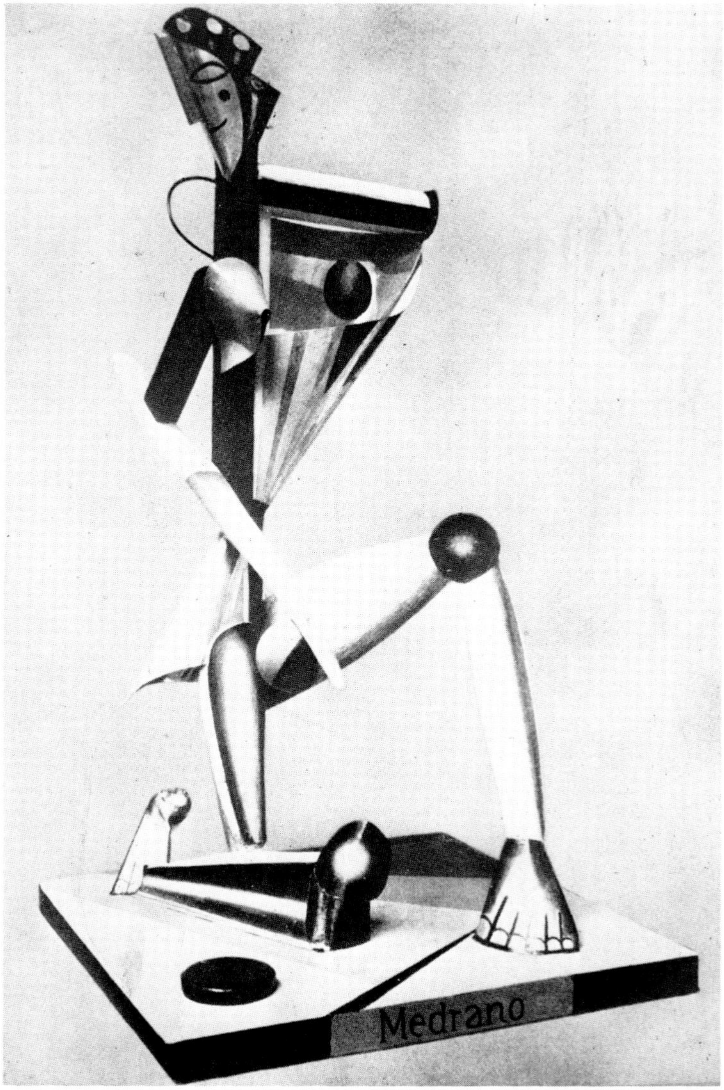

most renowned constructions, *Medrano II*,[11] and was exhibited as a Russian Futurist in an international survey of Futurist art in Rome.[12] The variety of the shows in which he participated, as well as the diversity of locations, suggest the vibrancy of Paris as a center for the international avant-garde while Archipenko was developing a personal direction for his art. Painters and sculptors came to the French capital from many European countries to explore various approaches to abstraction. Thus in the decade after his initial arrival in Paris, the sculptor gained recognition for his art, exhibited widely, instructed other young artists, and developed some of the sculptural innovations that were to sustain him up until the final creative years.

Having spent the war years in Cimiez, a suburb of Nice, in 1918 Archipenko undertook an ambitious tour of European cities; in Switzerland, England, Belgium, and Germany he exhibited his art. In 1920 a large solo exhibition of his work was included in the Biennale Exhibition in Venice. He married Angelica Bruno-Schmitz, a German sculptor, in 1921, and moved to Berlin where he opened an art school. In the same year, Archipenko's growing recognition in the United States was marked by his first one-man exhibition in this country, organized by the Société Anonyme (the first Museum of Modern Art) in New York,[13] and the publication of a monograph by Ivan Goll that was sponsored by the same institution.

By 1923 Archipenko had moved to the United States, and opened an art school in New York City. The next years were productive ones for the artist. He established a summer art school in Woodstock, New York in 1924. This program continued until the end of his life in nearby Bearsville, where he had purchased thirteen acres in 1929.

After his arrival in this country Archipenko set to work on his *Peinture Changeante* (or *Archipentura*), a motorized work that produced variable images in sequence (Fig. 3). The artist was granted a patent in 1927 for this kinetic invention that he dedicated to Thomas Edison and Albert Einstein. In 1928 Anderson Galleries held a one-man exhibition of the artist's sculptures, ceramics, sculpto-paintings, paintings, and drawings. Included in the catalogue for this exhibition was the artist's own description of *Archipentura*.[14]

In his discussion of this invention, Archipenko presented his ideas for a personal aesthetic that combined the scientific with the emotional. Designating *Archipentura* "an emotional creation, reflecting, by means of a new pictorial method, that phase of real life which cannot be rendered by means of static painting," he also called his invention

FIGURE 3

"the concrete union of painting with time and space."[15] The sculptor recalled that his *Medrano* of 1912 was an early attempt to record actual movement in a work of art, but this "animated painting" did not achieve the desired goal. In Germany in the early 1920s he became interested again in the problem of dynamism in modern art, but it was only in New York beginning in 1924 ". . . in the atmosphere of one of the most up-to-date cities in the world—that I succeeded."[16]

Confirming his declaration that *Archipentura* is "a superior form of art, containing within it life itself, since it paints energy,"[17] the other works in the 1928 show did not parallel this kinetic piece in inventiveness. One of the more striking examples to be included, however, was *Woman* of 1923 (Plate I-4) that had been purchased by Katherine Dreier, president of the Société Anonyme. Other than this construction in various metals, most of the sixty sculptures shown were in the traditional materials of bronze, marble, and ceramics, as were original plasters intended for casting. These works are indicative of Archipenko's style in the 1920s and later years. While some of the sculptural innovations of the teens continue in the following decades, there are generally more classically-inspired nudes, and few abstracted figures or constructed examples. The drawings of the middle years of Archipenko's career were in the manner of Michelangelo, harkening back to the copies he made of the Italian master's sketches as a youth.

While Archipenko became more concerned with classical purity and elegant surfaces in his middle years, the artist began to lecture widely on theories of creativity, and thus manifested that his personal inventiveness, and his desire to link art with the laws of nature, never slackened.

After the restrained elegance of the 1930s and 1940s, his use of a variety of industrial materials and his affinity for dazzling polychromy burst forth in a final display of virtuosity during the last decade of his life. From the early 1930s until the 1950s he lectured and taught art at numerous colleges and universities throughout the United States and Canada.[18] After the death of his first wife, Angelica, in 1957, Archipenko married Frances Gray, a sculptor and former student, in 1960. During the same year, many of the ideas that he presented on creativeness were finally published at length in his book *Archipenko, Fifty Creative Years*.[19] In this substantive volume were illustrated many of the impressive polychrome reliefs and sculpto-paintings of the immediately preceding decade which were juxtaposed with constructed examples from the Parisian period. The accompanying text provides a key to the interpretation of both. Archipenko wrote:

> *Early in my career, in the first decade of the century, I came to the conclusion that the spiritual power of a work of art is derived mostly from the metaphysical realm, that the greatest difficulty lies in the fixation of the correlation of abstract with material reality. Together they must evoke psychological and emotional reactions, the more the better, in order to lift the creator-artist and spectator into the realm of the sublime.*[20]

In other sections of this text, Archipenko summarized some of the principles of creativeness that he had presented frequently in illustrated lectures. He declared:

> *The artist knows that all creative causes within him are animated by cosmic dynamism which changes their combination to become the abstraction of matter or the concretion of abstract forces.*[21]

In seeking the inventive, the sculptor notes that this can be associated with nature's process of perceptual transformation from one thing to another. For Archipenko, therefore, the artmaking act was analogous to universal creativeness. He believed there was a continual evolutionary process that brought together cosmic energies with all matter, and that the artist was able to draw ideas from a cosmic creative force. His work is exemplary of this concern to join together the spiritual and material realms.

II. THEMES AND VARIATIONS

Archipenko's work of his last years is the culmination of the lifelong urge to create, and an embodiment of his personality. Many factors account for the form that his art was to take, including his innate creativity, the events of his life, and his continuous search for an appropriate form of personal expression.

The artist was keenly aware that he was criticized for the lack of a signature style, but he defended his approach to artmaking:

> *My diversity has often confused those critics who look for personality in the stereotyped production, while my personality is characterized by permanent change.*[22]

It is this continuity of change that can be explored through several themes in Archipenko's art—the standing figure, the reclining figure, sculptural groups and fragments, and the still life—and the variations he made of them throughout his career. The major portion of the artist's production eschews naturalism for various forms of abstraction. In addition to modernist approaches to the analysis of the forms of nature, the artist's Ukrainian heritage seems relevant to this affinity for abstraction. In the Ukraine there were indigenous cultures dating back to the Neolithic period; there were abstractions characterized by the interplay of line and mass. For subsequent cultures in this area, various precious metals were utilized in the creation of works of art. With the arrival of the Byzantine era there was an emphasis on the rhythmic repetition of line, and the use of dazzling color. All of these cultures have some importance to Archipenko.

In examining the artist's first sculptural works that he produced after coming to Paris, it is possible to distinguish his affinity with the art of primitive peoples (the ancient Americas and elsewhere) as well as the folk art tradition of his native country. His youthful experience watching works of the Greco-Scythian era being unearthed on archaeological digs in the Ukraine gave Archipenko an early attraction to the art of the ancient world. Sources for his early work can be found in archaic Greek sculpture, in the ancient idols that were to be discovered in the Ukraine, and in the African, Oceanic, and Meso-American artifacts found in French museums. A great eclectic, the artist was able to recast all of his source material into the development of a personal idiom.

An examination of his works in this show will also indicate the counterpoise that the artist achieved between the very old and the most recent. He was attracted to the Futurists and their attempts to represent the dynamism of the modern era. In addition to his invention of a machine for changing a pictorial image, Archipenko incorporated electric light into his sculpture while experimenting with such new materials as lucite and bakelite, and he eventually attached a motorized base to his sculpture to achieve actual motion (see *Revolving Figure*, Plate I-8). The sculptor hoped to bring the scientific and technological advancements of his age to visual form. He sincerely believed that the domains of the artist and the scientist were not so far removed from one another, and sought the universal principles that united both.

Sculpto-paintings and polychrome reliefs form the major portion of the current exhibition, and these works seem entirely representative of Archipenko's oeuvre. In addition, these works make appropriate examples for consideration of the artist's variations on a particular theme. The sustained interest in multi-media relief constructions by the artist attests to the significance that he attached to these works. In fact, Archipenko, in an essay of the 1920s, wrote that he considered the sculpto-paintings to be his most significant achievements.[23]

Variations on the subject of the standing female figure, for example, were often realized in sculpto-paintings which Archipenko invented in 1914 and defined as "a new character of art, due to its specific interdependencies of relief, concave or perforated forms, colors, or textures."[24] The artist felt that this artform was more adaptable to artistic invention than traditional painting and sculpture. The integral qualities of form and color were not only well-realized in these works, but sculpto-paintings were unlike previous relief sculpture in the history of art because of the use of new technical means and materials.

Michaelsen has stated that the artist made almost forty sculpto-paintings before 1920.[25] Another concentration of these works appears in the late 1950s. Archipenko viewed these works as the most appropriate means of joining color with form, and since the artist was a major advocate of polychromy in sculpture, this unity of the pictorial and the plastic was an achievement of major importance to his personal aesthetic. In these examples he projected volumes for figural elements and considered their dynamic interplay with pictorial surfaces. The sculptor was even conscious of variations in the intensity and direction of light sources, and considered the manner in which the shadows could become an integral part of the composition. He recognized that, due to its use of methods and materials of the contemporary era, sculpto-painting intensified the optical and esthetic effect of form. Noting the limitations of other forms of art-making, Archipenko regarded the sculpto-painting as offering an excellent possibility for meaning. He stated:

> *Sculpto-painting is more effective and diverse in character than the usual painting or uncolored sculpture. The unification of color and form does not interfere with spiritualization; on the contrary, it facilitates the expression of the abstract in this medium.*[26]

In the last decade of his life, Archipenko returned to the sculpto-painting, fully utilizing the expressive possibilities inherent in his invention. In addition to these mixed-media pieces, the artist made bronze castings of some of the lost works from his Parisian years. In the few examples of reliefs that were modeled after sculpto-paintings, various patinas have been employed to simulate the original polychrome surfaces. Since these bronze reliefs are closely related to the integration of the two-dimensional and the three-dimensional as found in the sculpto-paintings, they seem appropriate to consider here. In all instances it is the effect of light and shadow on the plastically-realized elements which becomes integral to the artist's aesthetic.

Archipenko's drawings and prints have a varied position within his oeuvre. While he produced sketches throughout his life, they do not always relate to his sculptural production. The artist noted that the direct approach and spontaneity that gave "vital character" to the sculpto-paintings and constructions[27] came about because he did not make preliminary studies. For direct carving or construction in obdurate materials, however, the sculptor did make color studies.

Noting the rush of ideas and feelings that come to an artist before the actual completion of a sculpture, Archipenko thus explained the hasty sketches—sometimes no more than a few incisive lines—with which he filled innumerable notebooks. *Les Formes Vivantes* prints produced at St. Gallen, Switzerland, for example, began as a series of rapid sketches. There are other drawings that are intended to provoke the memory or stimulate the mind, and record works (or ideas) in progress.

The drawings included in the discussion of themes and variations, however, fit into another category that is distinguishable, according to the artist, because

> *. . . the essence remains in its transformative character, which evolves into a style expressive of the personality of the artist, through specific forms, lines, patterns, and techniques.*[28]

And what do these works reveal about the personality of the artist? I believe that, through the polychrome reliefs and related works on paper, Archipenko appears as an artist with an inquiring mind who sought to communicate his ideas about the nature of life. He had a remarkable determination about his personal direction in artmaking despite frequent criticism. He was a loner who defied convention, and tried to withstand all practical hardships in order to pursue his art. He taught and lectured in order to support himself, but his financial struggle did not discourage his will to create. While he must have experienced disappointment in his life, his artistic energy continued unabated.

Finally, in the years immediately preceding and following his marriage to Frances Gray, Archipenko's most resplendent and dynamic works in decades appeared. In these years the deep spirituality inherent in his work, as well as his indebtedness to his cultural origins, was most in evidence. The production of the sculptor's later years includes remarkably fresh variations on the major themes he represented throughout his career.

Standing Figures

This theme is one of the most frequently found in the production of Archipenko, and already appears in his early years in Paris. At various times the standing figure assumes different significances for the artist. Within the reliefs and sculpto-paintings included here, for example, the artist presents the figure as coquette, as classical goddess, as primitive idol, as Madonna, or as dancer. Invariably the standing figure is female.

In *Woman with Fan* (Plate IV-12) and *Woman with Fan II* (Plate I-2), Archipenko created a Cubist version of a female nude posed flirtatiously for the spectator. These figures, while sensuous, have the mechanistic appearance and sharp angularities of the Cubo-Futurist style. In *Woman with Fan II* there is a certain visual appeal in the pure spectral hues, but the possible eroticism of the curving torso and rounded hips of this nude is countered by the interplay of sharply-defined geometric elements in the composition.

Woman, 1923 (Plate I-4), is a culmination of Archipenko's Cubist period, and the most machine-like of his works in appearance. This relief was constructed in a variety of metals that substitute for the polychromy of the earlier work. Here the curving outline of the female form remains, but because of the copper, brass, and silver components, the work also gives the appearance of a turbine. The machinomorphic figures produced by Oskar Schlemmer in the early 1920s in Germany parallel this construction.

After the many freestanding female figures in stone, bronze, and lucite of the 1930s and 1940s, Archipenko again returned to the standing figure in mixed-media reliefs during the 1950s. *Venus*, 1954 (Plate I-7), and *Oceanic Madonna* (Fig. 4, p. 17) are two examples that use an array of decorative materials in the manner of a Russian icon. Like those religious works in which jewel-encrusted surfaces attest to the sanctity and preciousness of the image, the two reliefs include mirrors and mother-of-pearl mosaics to form a rich, decorative effect. *Venus*, an abstract—seemingly hooded—figure, is sensuous because of its dazzling textures and colors rather than its anatomical illusions.

FIGURE 4

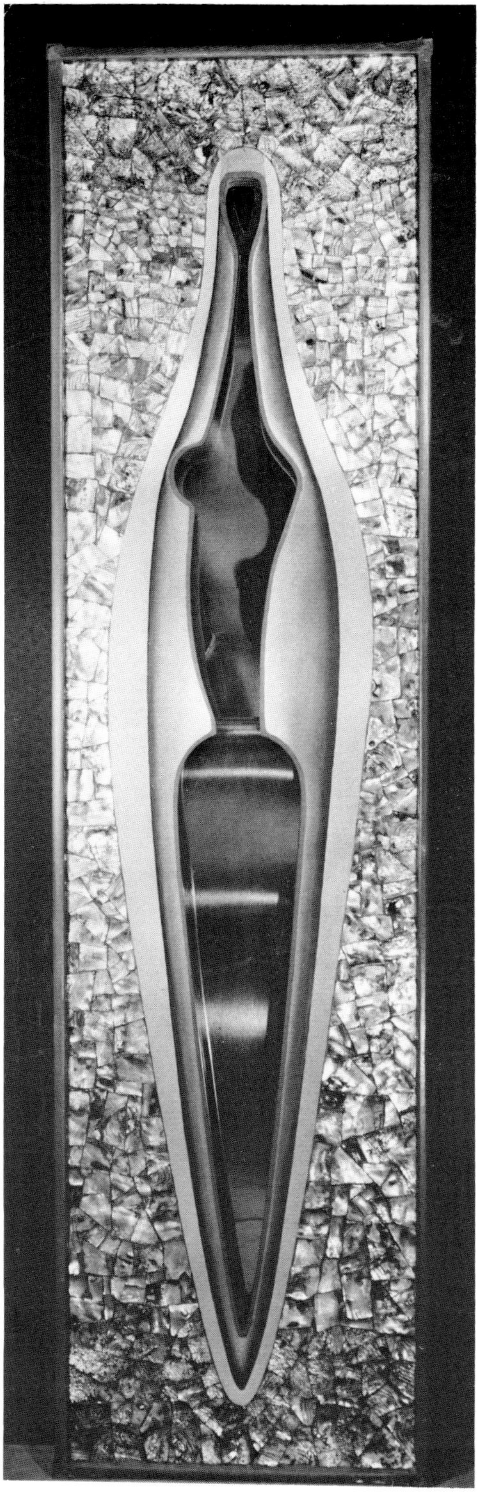

Multi-colored Figure, 1957 (Plate I-9), is the culmination of the secular icons that were created by Archipenko. This figure, encased in a shell-like structure of many hues, seems derived from the Byzantine tradition in its stylized forms and emphasis on flat shapes. However, organic allusions are also suggested here.

Archipenko combined modern and traditional styles; he derived his art from the great ages of the past as well as from the contemporary era. The theme of the standing figure is exemplary of the range of his sources. The subject appears in the initial phases of his artistic production when he is influenced by primitive art and Cubism, and survives until the final years in the decorative examples found here.

Reclining Figures

This theme is among the most traditional subjects in the history of art. Reclining nude figures are found in the ancient world, and they are a particular favorite of Renaissance artists. The theme can suggest the beauty of all creation as well as the idealization of the female. Representations in the past have stressed either the eroticism of the body or the absolute perfection of the feminine form.

In Archipenko's use of this theme, beginning in the 1930s, the reclining female is almost always represented as a floating torso. These ethereal creatures are stylized fragments of the body, as if reminiscent of archaeological discoveries from the ancient world. In these and in many other examples, the sculptor effectively uses the fragmentary form as a splendid vehicle of expression.

Torso in Space (Plate II-1) is an image that recurs through the artist's oeuvre of the middle and late years. In the bronze examples that the artist produced in various sizes during the 1930s, the simplified torso is extended above narrow supports so that the curves of the female form can be visualized in their entirety. These sculptures are primarily frontal, and thus closely related to the later collages and sculpto-paintings. Two collages of the 1950s (Plates II-3 and II-4) are abstractions of a more fully realized pictorial version of a floating torso that appeared as a lithograph in 1952 (Plate II-2). In the latter example, the presence of another figure behind the torso suggests the maidservant in Manet's *Olympia*—or is an admirer of the reclining nude. These pictorial illusions are abandoned in the collages where bold contrasts of color and form stress the two-dimensional surface as an abstract pattern.

Cleopatra (Plate II-5) is Archipenko's most impressive late variation on the theme of the reclining figure. The "Queen of the Nile" complete with found objects and brilliantly-hued curving elements brings the sensuality of his earlier torsos to a more developed expression.

Still Life

A few examples of the still life are included in the current exhibition, and most of these images appeared during the teens. Reliefs and polychrome bronzes that appear in the 1950s are derived from the compositions from the Cubist period. Among all of the subjects considered here, the still life is the most exemplary of Archipenko's straightforward interpretation of a static, traditional, compositional type into the fluid dynamism of Cubist collage. Like the *papiers collés* and collages of Picasso and Braque that inspired Archipenko's initial constructions and sculpto-paintings, these still life arrangements introduce a variety of angular and curving shapes into a tightly-interlocking composition. Many of the contours of individual objects remain intact as they do in the remarkable still life paintings by Juan Gris. Like the other Cubist masters, Archipenko also employs fragments of objects or characteristic textures or patterns to abstractly represent certain components of the arrangement.

While the still life theme can be connected to the academic tradition through the ages, the constructions of Archipenko link time and space, and share in the more energetic abstractions of this subject that appear in the modern era.

Group Figures and Fragmentary Figures

One of the preferred subjects of Archipenko, particularly in the late years, is the multi-figured composition. Works on paper, bronze reliefs, and sculpto-paintings are to be found in this category, and some of the most innovative achievements of the 1950s are included. A few examples are similar to archaeological fragments arranged on a flat surface. Bronze reliefs on marble slabs such as Eagle, 1959 (Plate IV-11), *Conversation*, 1959 (Plate IV-8), and *Fragmentary Relief*, 1959 (Plate IV-10), are examples. These varied pieces of bronze form stylized renditions of the human body, while the richly variegated markings in the marble surface serve to unify the composition. While some of these reliefs suggest the juxtaposition of energetic figures engaged in a dialogue, others evoke a biblical or mythological narrative.

In 1957 Archipenko produced a number of polychromed wood and bakelite sculpto-paintings. A number of these are fragmented figures, showing the artist's experimentation with the concave and convex, vivid color and textural variations and the integration of solid and mass. At times there is an ambiguity in the formation of a figural component as distinct from the surrounding space. It is this manipulation of space that is essential to Archipenko's personal aesthetic. He wrote:

> *According to my experience, this concept of modeling the form of space is based primarily on symbolic, associative, and esthetic qualities. This becomes a creative process which may be compared with the psychological reconstruction of the absent object reposing in our memory. A meaningless pierced hole can never become a proper symbol. In art the shape of the empty space should be no less significant than the meaning of the shape of the solid matter. . . . Through the modulation of space our consciousness participates in the creative process because that which does not exist is recreated within us in the abstract form of space, and becomes a reality in our optical memory. . . . I believe that the whole biological evolution of the human being and the progress of civilization is based exclusively on this creative power of nature in producing that which is not there.*[29]

Thus it can be understood that the principal aim of Archipenko's art was giving visual expression to the basic laws of nature—to the pulsating energies that join all forms of life. At the same time his works are deeply connected with the artist himself, his cultural heritage, and the experiences of his life. In the examples of his late years included in this exhibition, Archipenko can be seen as returning to the sculptural considerations of his youth in another period of remarkable inventiveness. In these polychrome reliefs, sculpto-paintings and related works on paper, he realized the culmination of his life as an artist, and successfully unified spirit and matter to produce associations related to nature and all human experiences.

Joan Marter

ENDNOTES

[1]The author wishes to express her sincere thanks to Frances Archipenko Gray for the use of materials from the Archipenko archives in Bearsville, New York. Katherine J. Michaelsen generously supplied information on specific works. The staff of the Watson Library at the Metropolitan Museum of Art should be acknowledged for assistance with the research for this publication.

[2]See, for example: Hilton Kramer, "The Innovations of Archipenko," *The New York Times,* May 14, 1967. The critic stated, "For myself, the late sculptures are—to say the least—problematic. But there are in the U.C.L.A. show, a series of lithographs from the nineteen-sixties that are stunning in their masculine force and clarity."

[3]Frederick S. Wight, "Alexander Archipenko, Life and Work" in: UCLA Art Galleries, *Alexander Archipenko* (Los Angeles: Ward Ritchie Press, 1967), p. 26. Wight also stated: "For Archipenko does achieve his final breakthrough in his last ten years."

[4]Alexander Archipenko, *Archipenko, Fifty Creative Years 1908-1958.* New York: Tekhne, 1960, p. 18.

[5]Hans Hildebrandt, *Alexander Archipenko,* (Berlin: Ukrainske Slowo, 1923), p. 6.

[6]*Ibid,* p. 7. "Thus a very strong and unexpected impression which Archipenko received when in Moscow, brought about a decided turn . . . An exhibition of the works of French painters and sculptors of the Impressionistic School revealed to the 20-year-old youth much of the realm of living art."

[7]For details on Archipenko's Parisian years, including the controversy about the date of his arrival there see: Katherine Michaelsen, *Archipenko: A Study of the Early Work.* (New York: Garland Press, 1977), pp. 4-10.

[8]Additional information on multi-media construction can be found in: Katherine J. Michaelsen, "Early Mixed-Media Constructions," *Arts Magazine,* 50 (January 1976), pp. 72-76. For discussion of *Medrano I* as a seminal work, see: Donald Karshan, *Archipenko* (Boulder: Westview Press, 1975), pp. 11-16.

[9]Umberto Boccioni, "Technical Manifesto of Futurist Sculpture" in Umbro Apollonio, ed., *Futurist Manifestos* (New York: Viking Press, 1970), pp. 51-65. In this document Boccioni declared that sculptors should "Insist that even twenty different types of materials can be used in a single work of art in order to achieve plastic movement. To mention a few examples: glass, wood, cardboard, iron, cement, hair, leather, cloth, mirrors, electric lights, etc." Archipenko developed a friendship with Gino Severini, an Italian Futurist living in Paris, and he must have been attracted to Futurist concepts of "environmental sculpture" in which the dynamic relationship between the piece and the space it occupies is explored. The Italians also promoted the idea of kinetic sculpture which would correspond to the motion of machines. Therefore, Futurist concepts joined with Archipenko's earlier exposure to the collages of Picasso and Braque to influence his interest in multi-media constructions and sculpto-paintings.

[10]For a detailed discussion of Archipenko's exhibition history during the Parisian years see: Katherine J. Michaelsen, *Archipenko,* pp. 4-10.

[11]*Medrano II,* a circus dancer, is now in the collection of the Solomon R. Guggenheim Museum. *Medrano I* (destroyed) was completed by October of 1912, and exhibited in Budapest in 1913. Although the work was signed and dated 1915, it was exhibited at the Salon des Indépendants in 1914 and illustrated in *L'Intransigeant,* March 2, 1914. For a photograph of *Medrano II* as installed at the Salon des Indépendants among Russian Cubo-Futurist paintings see: Karshan, *op. cit.,* p. 16.

[12]Roma, Galleria Sprovieri, "Esposizione Libera Futurista Internazionale," Galleria Sprovieri, April 13-May 25, 1914.

[13]New York, Gallery of Société Anonyme, February 1-March 15, 1921. In this first solo exhibition of Archipenko in the United States, six watercolors, eight sculptures, and seven sculpto-paintings were shown. In 1924 another Archipenko exhibition was sponsored by the Société Anonyme at the Kingore Gallery, New York. This show

included thirty sculptures and six sculpto-paintings. The catalogue introduction was written by Christian Brinton.

[14]New York, Anderson Galleries, "Archipenko: Catalogue of Exhibition and Description of 'Archipentura,' " (1928), pp. .

[15]*Ibid.*, p. 3.

[16]*Ibid.*, pp. 3-4.

[17]*Ibid.*, p. 4. For another discussion of *Archipentura* see: *Fifty Creative Years*, pp. 65-66.

[18]For a list of the fourteen institutions where Archipenko taught and 53 lectures he presented at colleges and universities see: Archipenko, *Fifty Creative Years*, p. 95.

[19]A tape recording of a lecture given by Archipenko in Winnipeg, Manitoba, Canada, January 15, 1962 is available at the Archives of American Art, Smithsonian Institution, Washington, D.C. Notes for Archipenko's lectures are included in the Archipenko Papers, 1912-1966, Archives of American Art, NA 1-NA 25.

[20]Archipenko, *Fifty Creative Years*, p. 35.

[21]*Ibid.*, p. 21.

[22]*Ibid.*, p. 20.

[23]Frankfurt-am-Main, Kunstsalon Ludwig Schames, "Alexander Archipenko—Lyonel Feininger," May, 1922. For a discussion of the sculpto-paintings see Michaelsen, *Archipenko*, pp. 126-145.

[24]Archipenko, *Fifty Creative Years*, p. 40.

[25]Michaelsen, *Archipenko*, p. 127.

[26]Archipenko, *Fifty Creative Years*, p. 41.

[27]*Ibid.*, p. 63.

[28]*Ibid.*

[29]*Ibid.*, pp. 57-58.

I. STANDING FIGURES

I-1

BATHER, 1915

Oil & pencil on metal, wood, and paper

20 × 11½″

Collection: Philadelphia Museum of Art, Louise and Walter Arensberg Collection

Archipenko's *Bather* is a well-known and representative example of his early work in sculpto-painting, a medium which he invented in 1914.[1] Derived from the formal vocabulary of Cubist painting, the sculpto-paintings involved not only painterly qualities of coloration and illusionism, but also sculptural concerns with the modelling and arrangement of actual three-dimensional forms in relief. Of this blending of media, Archipenko wrote: "The nuances of form and color and their interdependencies are as essential and significant as the nuances of sound and silence in music. No boundary can be drawn between color and real form because esthetically and technically they are reciprocally integrated. We see that nature never separates form from color but, from different causes, unites them in infinite variety."[2]

In the *Bather,* a woman holding a towel steps from a tub. Her body is tightly knit with the forms of her environment through the use of interlocking conic sections. This arrangement of cones, Archipenko's idiosyncratic version of Cubist faceting, produces a tight yet dynamic composition.

I-2

WOMAN WITH FAN II, 1915

Painted wood relief

19½ × 15¾″

Collection: Hirshhorn Museum and Sculpture Garden

This sculpto-painting is Archipenko's second version of a popular Cubist subject.[3] The earlier work, *Woman with a Fan* of 1914, is his earliest surviving sculpto-painting,[4] and appears in a later bronze version in Plate IV-12.

Although the architectural setting in this piece is more complex than in *Bather* (Plate I-1), emphasis is placed on the female figure rather than the pictorial structure as a whole. Illusionistic devices thrust the woman into the foreground, at a discernible spatial remove from the elements which surround her. The rendering of her body with sinuous curves further differentiates her from the straight-edged and orthogonal stairs, platforms, and pillars. This virtuoso treatment displays Archipenko's sensitivity to the female form, his favorite subject throughout his *oeuvre*. Despite the extreme stylization and abstraction of body parts, the woman with the fan retains a frankly erotic quality. This sensuality is further enhanced by the warm, gently modelled colors with which she is painted.

I-4

WOMAN (METAL LADY), 1923
Brass, copper, wood, and new silver
54½ × 20½″
Collection: Yale University Art Gallery

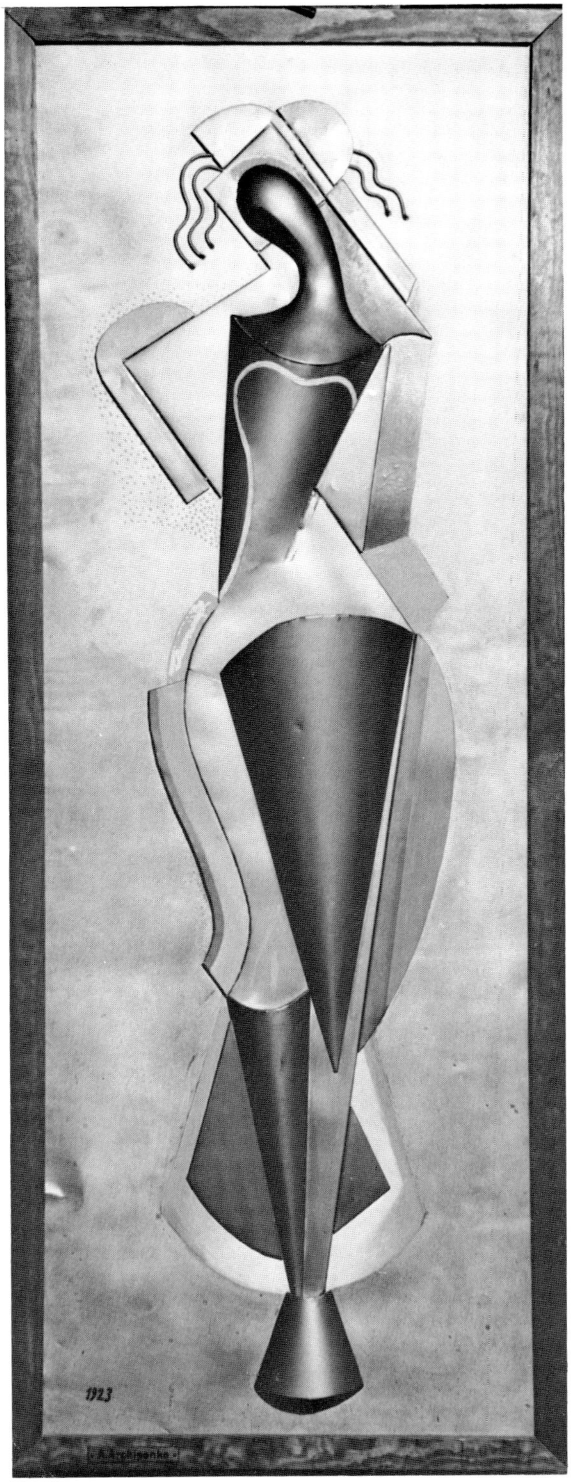

Formally related to many lithographs and sculpto-paintings of the period, the *Metal Lady* represents an innovation in medium: the relief is constructed almost totally of metal. This feature perhaps determined the work's inclusion in the seminal Machine Age Exposition held at New York's Little Gallery in 1927. Archipenko wrote an accompanying statement for the show's catalogue in which he declared, "It is indisputable that the basis of Art always remains the same, even though the exterior forms of Art change, the spirit of the epochs is reflected in these forms. . . . Let us take the present epoch—The Machine Age. If we were not so close to it today, and if we could see with an eye embracing many centuries at one time, it would be easy for us to distinguish that the present period is the time of Machine and Action."[7]

The *Metal Lady*'s presence in this show, as well as in the Société Anonyme collection, has made it Archipenko's best-known work in America, after his ubiquitously reproduced *Woman Combing Her Hair* (1915).

I-5

FIGURE, 1917 (1930s?)
Painted wood relief
27 × 20½″
Collection: Frances Archipenko Gray

The design of this severely abstracted human form was reproduced by Archipenko in an oil painting of 1938,[8] and it is possible that this sculpto-painting was executed at the same time. Both works, however, may derive from a common image originally conceived in 1917. One characteristic which justifies a later dating is the figure's lack of strong gender-specific qualities. In the late teens, Archipenko worked exclusively with representations of female figures, and rendered them with obviously feminine breasts and hips. Not until the mid-1930s did his human forms become more sexually ambiguous.

I-6

RELIEF, 1936 (1950s?)
Aluminum
43¼ × 9¼"
Collection: Frances Archipenko Gray

One of eight casts, *Relief* is based on, and may have been cast from, a work entitled *Plaster Relief* of 1936. The aluminum version may not have been created until sometime in the 1950's, for it was not exhibited until 1960, while its plaster predecessor was shown in a major retrospective in 1954.[9]

The figure in *Relief,* composed entirely of curvilinear forms, is not only sexually ambivalent but ambiguous as regards species as well. Its upright posture and foot provide its only anthropomorphic elements. This sort of biomorph may have been inspired by the nonspecific organisms created by the Surrealists, whose works were then gaining popularity in America.

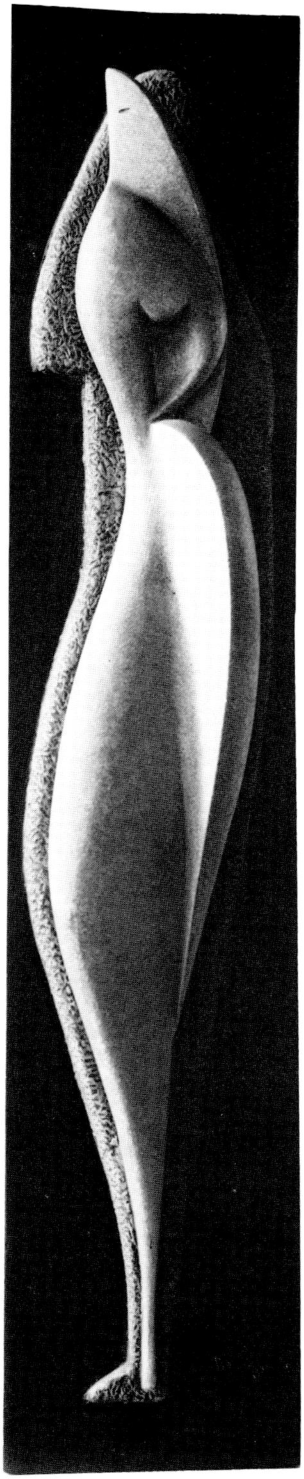

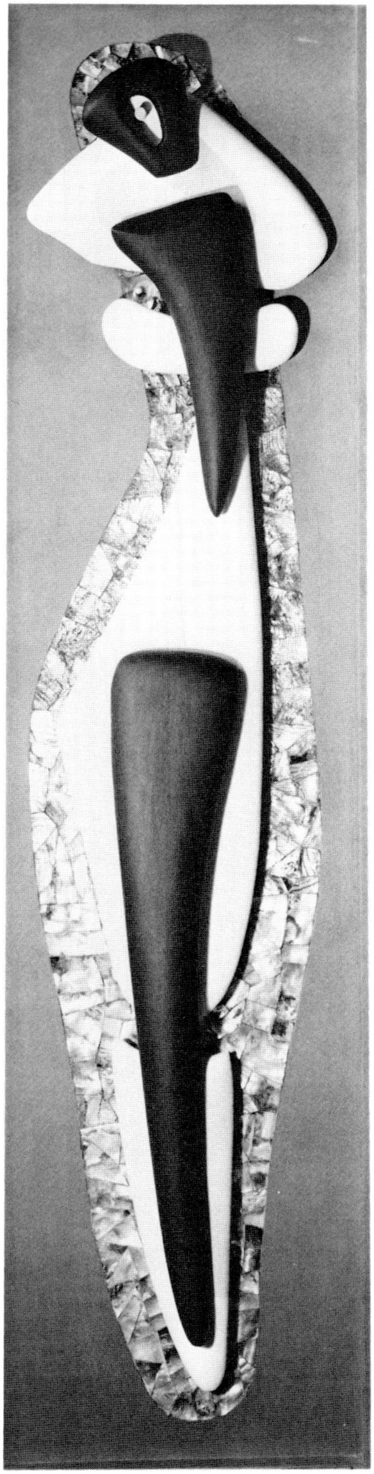

I-7
VENUS, 1953
Wood, mother of pearl mosaic
60″ high
Collection: Frances Archipenko Gray

Venus, another biomorphic image, seems more human than *Relief* (Plate I-6). Its title implies a female figure, an implication reinforced by formal allusions to a head, breasts, and hips. Archipenko explained this vague ontogeny-within-phylogeny approach thus: "We as human beings are creatively connected with every organic and non-organic thing in the universe. In view of this fact, the creative artist that I am, I use these forces to express them through the forms."[10]

The mosaic pattern which holds the figure together is not Archipenko's first application of that medium. He had worked in mosaic in the 1920s, producing works such as *Torso in Ceramic and Mosaic* (1928).[11]

I-8

REVOLVING FIGURE, 1956

Wood, mother of pearl mosaic, formica, metal
78″ high
Collection: Frances Archipenko Gray

This work, constructed of two intersecting planar figures, has four surfaces, each covered with a different material: wood, mother of pearl mosaic, formica, and metal. Archipenko was interested in the reflective qualities of these surfaces, and their interactions with one another and their environment. Since 1914, when a real mirror was used in his construction *Woman in Front of a Mirror*, the artist had explored the properties of reflection.[12] Concerning this phenomenon, he wrote, "Reflection enriches the effect of the object. It can multiply lines; it can amplify or reduce the effect of forms, color, or line; it can transform shape according to the positions of the planes or the concave or convex bending of the reflecting metal. Reflections express depth and space; they absorb the environment to which they are exposed; they magnify the brilliance of color."[13] In *Revolving Figure* these effects are made even more rich and complex as the sculpture turns through space, reflecting varying intensities of illumination on its different faces.

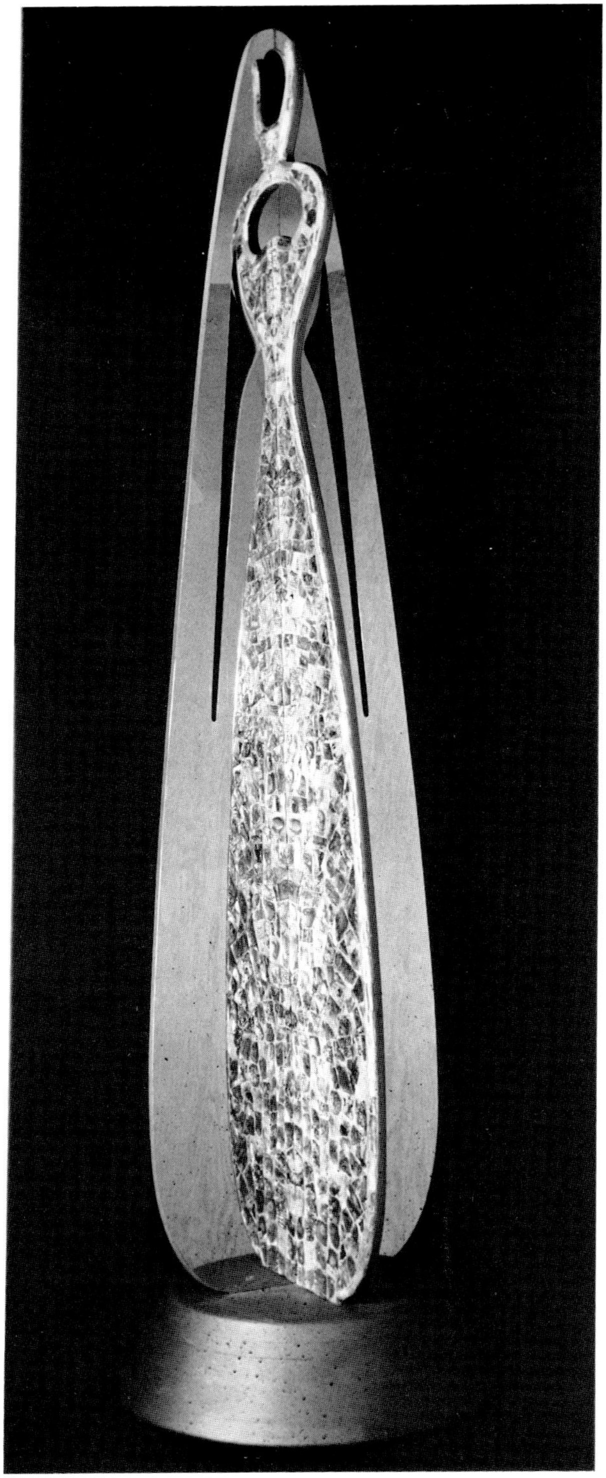

I-9
MULTI-COLORED FIGURE, 1957
Wood, metal, bakelite
52×26″
Collection: Frances Archipenko Gray

This sculpto-painting was also produced for the Perls Gallery show. As in *Ballerina* (Plate I-10) the relief's outer portions are ambiguous. Either the biomorphic figure is large and imposing, unified by its cross-hatched sides, or it is thin, weak, and segmented, protected by a seed- or womb-like structure.

I-10

BALLERINA, 1957

Wood and metal

24 × 14″

Collection: Frances Archipenko Gray

Ballerina was first exhibited in Archipenko's 1957 Perls Gallery show, for which he rejuvenated the medium of sculpto-painting.[14] He had not worked consistently with polychromed reliefs since the early 1920s. Constructed of slender biomorphs in a manner similar to Venus (Plate I-7), the figure is surrounded by curvilinear forms which may or may not be integral parts of its anatomy. This enclosing element appears time and again in Archipenko's late reliefs and drawings.

Archipenko also produced a smaller version of *Ballerina* in the same year.[15]

II. RECLINING FIGURES

II-1
TORSO IN SPACE, 1936
Bronze
60″ long
Collection: Frances Archipenko Gray

A life-sized bronze, *Torso in Space* was preceded by two smaller versions (22½ inches long) cast the previous year. While the large piece has a relatively dull finish, the smaller ones are plated with gold and chromium respectively, which gives them gleaming reflective surfaces.[16] These three works mark the beginning of Archipenko's interest in reclining nudes. This particular formal treatment of the female body, however, can be traced to works of the teens. Upright figures such as *Black Torso* (1913), and *White Torso* (1916), display the same truncated body, smooth surface, and elimination of anatomical detail.[17]

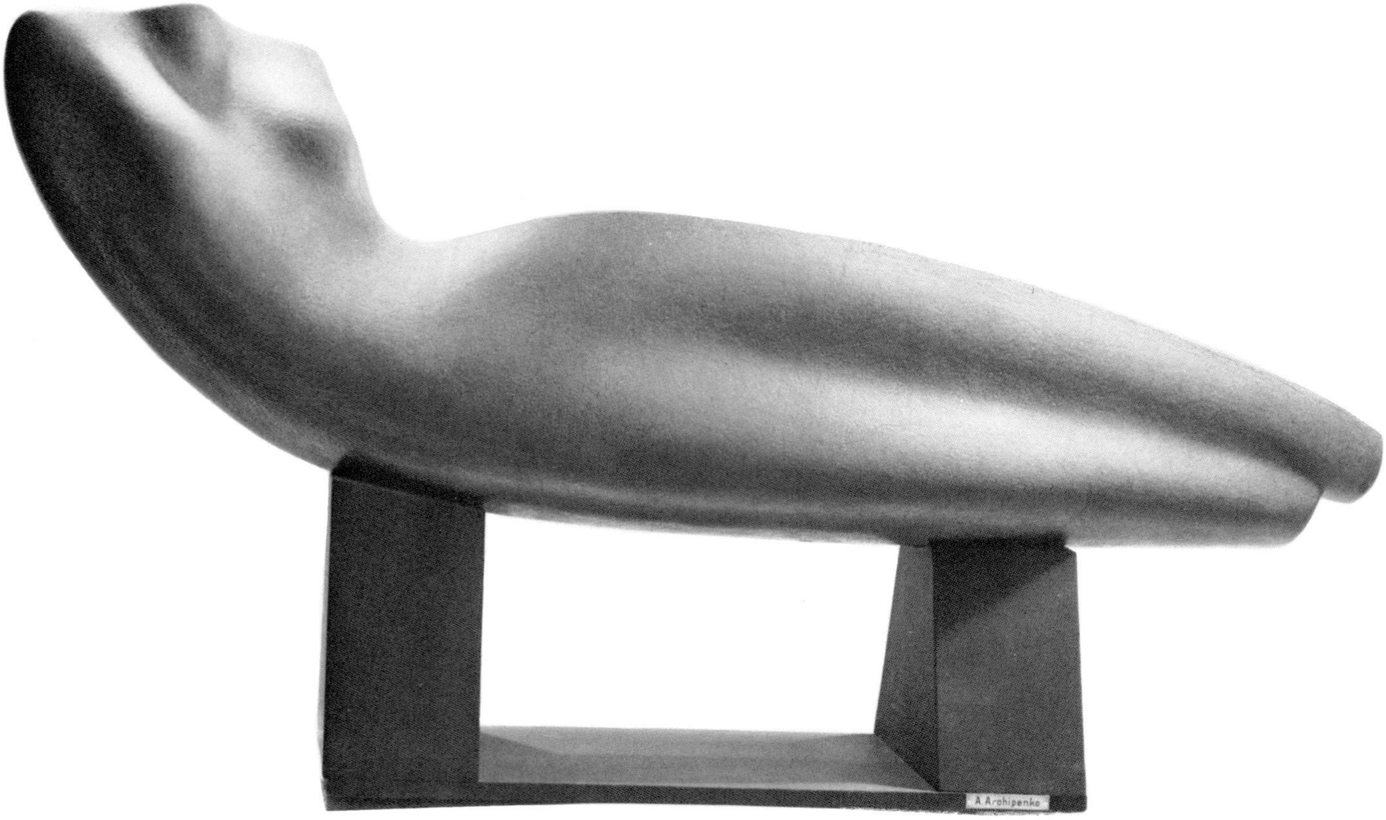

In this multi-media print, the abstracted female form of the sculptural *Torso in Space* of 1935-1936 (Plate II-1) is featured in a composition fraught with ambiguities. The familiar figure rests upon a biomorphic field which, at second glance, seems to be the figure's outer portion, owing to suggestions of an elbow, head, and hand at the upper left. This situation is further complicated by the dark form which looms on the right. Is this a separate, distinct figure, or merely a shadow or reflection of the reclining woman? The confusion is ultimately unresolvable, and produces a mysterious, tense, and foreboding image.

II-2
TORSO IN SPACE, 1952
Lithography, serigraphy, embossing
24¾ × 14 7/8″
Edition of 50
Collection: Frances Archipenko Gray

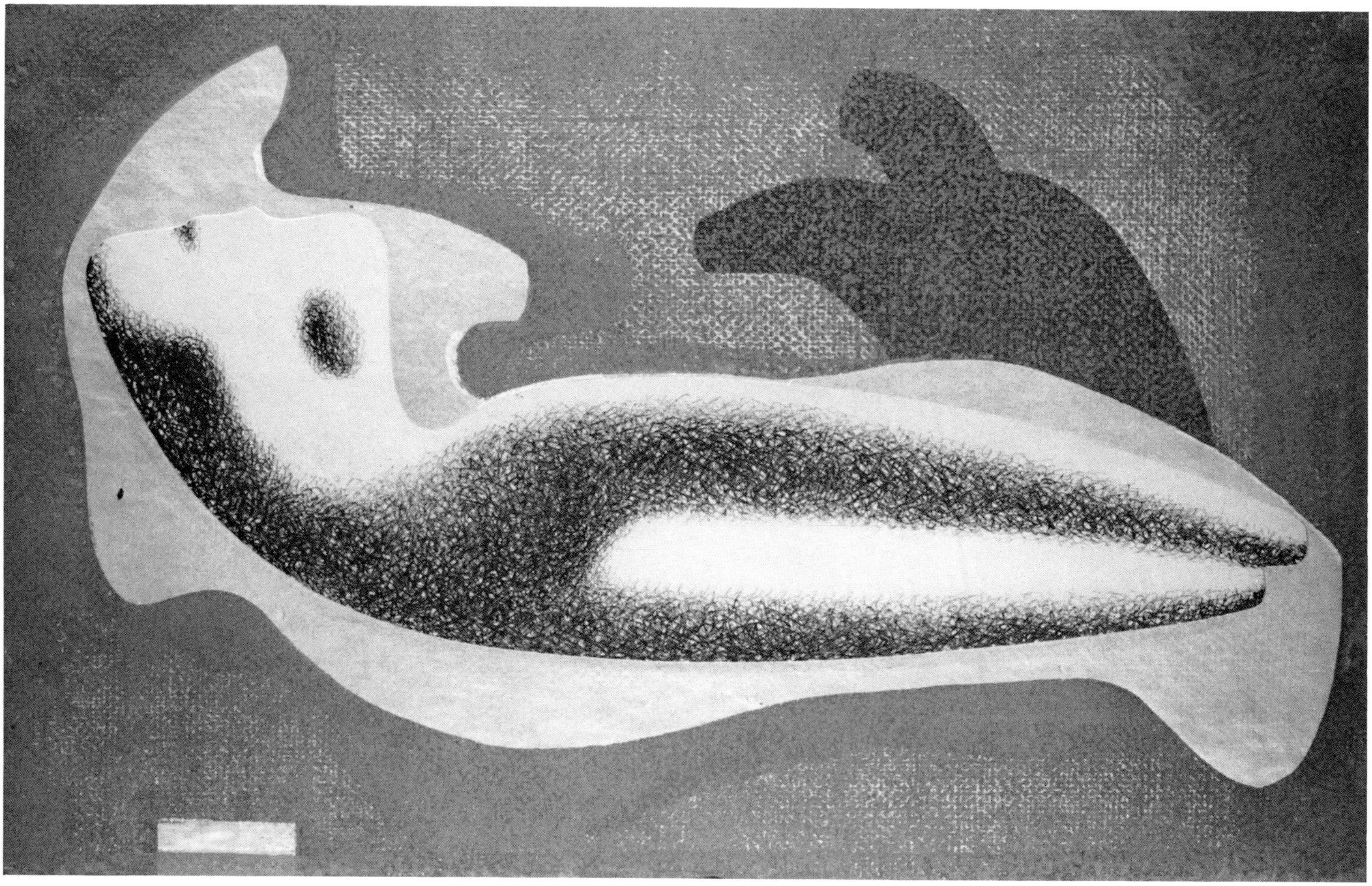

II-3
COLLAGE (TORSO), 1953
Collage with perforated surface, wood, paper
18×24″
Collection: Frances Archipenko Gray

Although Archipenko's writing on collage stressed its utility as a preliminary sketch for sculptural projects,[18] the two works that follow are finished art objects which derived ultimately from sculpture. In these collages the two torso forms are not used expressionistically, as in the *Torso in Space* print (Plate II-2), but as elements in carefully ordered patterns which border on the decorative. In the 1953 collage, the patterning effect is achieved through a repetition and variation of the curves of the torso. The body in the later piece acts as a segment in an interlocking surface pattern which unites figure and ground in a manner reminiscent of Archipenko's Cubist sculpto-paintings, (see Plate I-1).

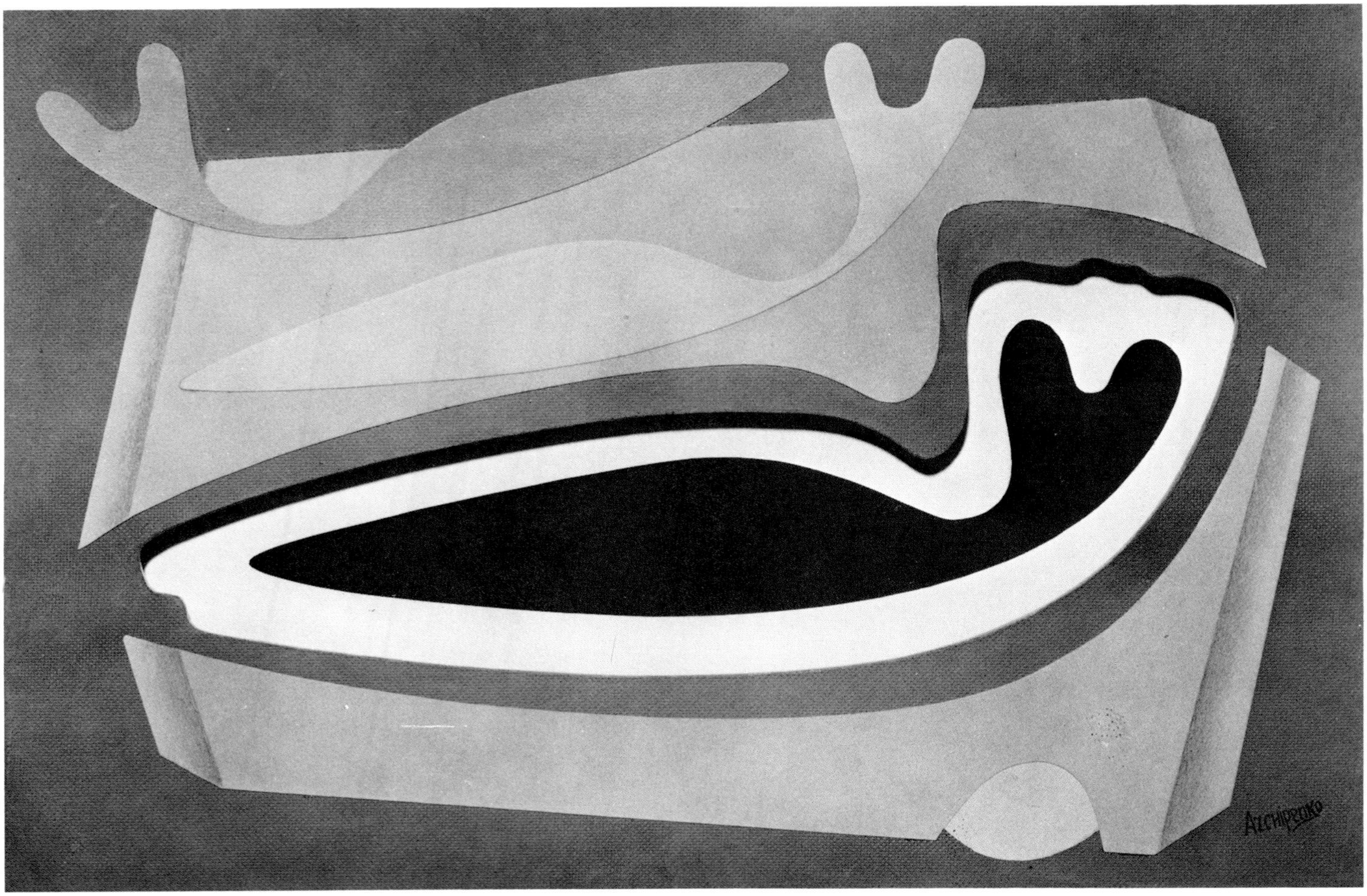

II-4
COLLAGE (TORSO), 1954
Collage with perforated surface,
wood, metal
18 × 28″
Collection: Frances Archipenko Gray

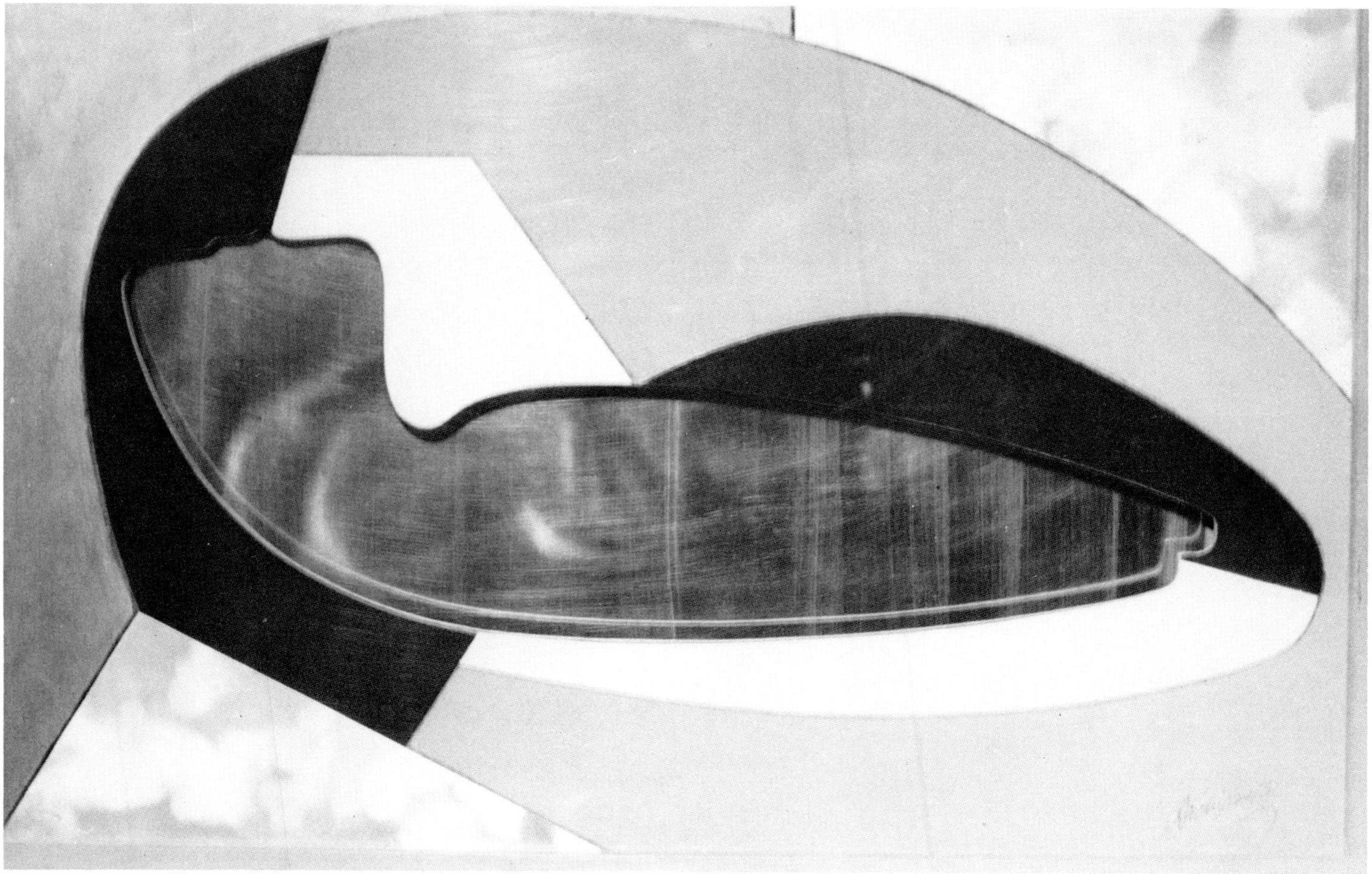

II-5
CLEOPATRA, (REPOSE), 1957
Wood, bakelite, polychrome
38×84″
Collection: Frances Archipenko Gray

The largest of his 1957 sculpto-paintings, and the largest reclining figure in his *oeuvre*, *Cleopatra* is a work which incorporates many of Archipenko's most important artistic traits and innovations. The figure, characteristically female, is constructed of ambiguous biomorphic sections. She is integrated into the composition through a system of convex and concave forms, the manipulation of which is probably Archipenko's greatest contribution to the history of sculpture. Also present is the artist's concern for reflection, manifested in the mirror image of the queen's head, and his love of intricate surface patterns, as seen in the accentuated wood grain which no doubt represents the Nile. To the immediate right of *Cleopatra*'s head three small objects are affixed: a coral necklace, a silver bracelet, and a stone. Such found objects appeared in Archipenko's work as early as 1912.[19] These elements all combine to create a sumptuous image of elegance, vanity, and decadence.

In 1927, Archipenko painted an oil titled *Cleopatra*, but it has little in common with the 1957 sculpto-painting. The earlier piece depicts a naturalistic, if somewhat stocky, nude seated woman with no particularly queenly attributes.[20]

The following two figures (Plates II-6, II-7) recline, and seem to be female, but they are not in the direct formal line of reclining figures begun with the *Torso in Space* and climaxed with *Cleopatra* (see Plate II-1 –II-5). Their massive, agitated bodies seem to derive from two disparate tendencies. The first is Archipenko's fascination with bulky women, as manifested in his drawings and graphic work from the teens and 1920s (see Plate I-3). The second is a looser handling of paint and pencil seen in many of his two-dimensional works in the 1950s and early 1960s. In combination, the result is severely abstracted, quaking, powerful figures which arouse strange emotional responses.

II-6
FIGURE, 1960
Colored pencil & tempera
28 × 22″
Collection: Frances Archipenko Gray

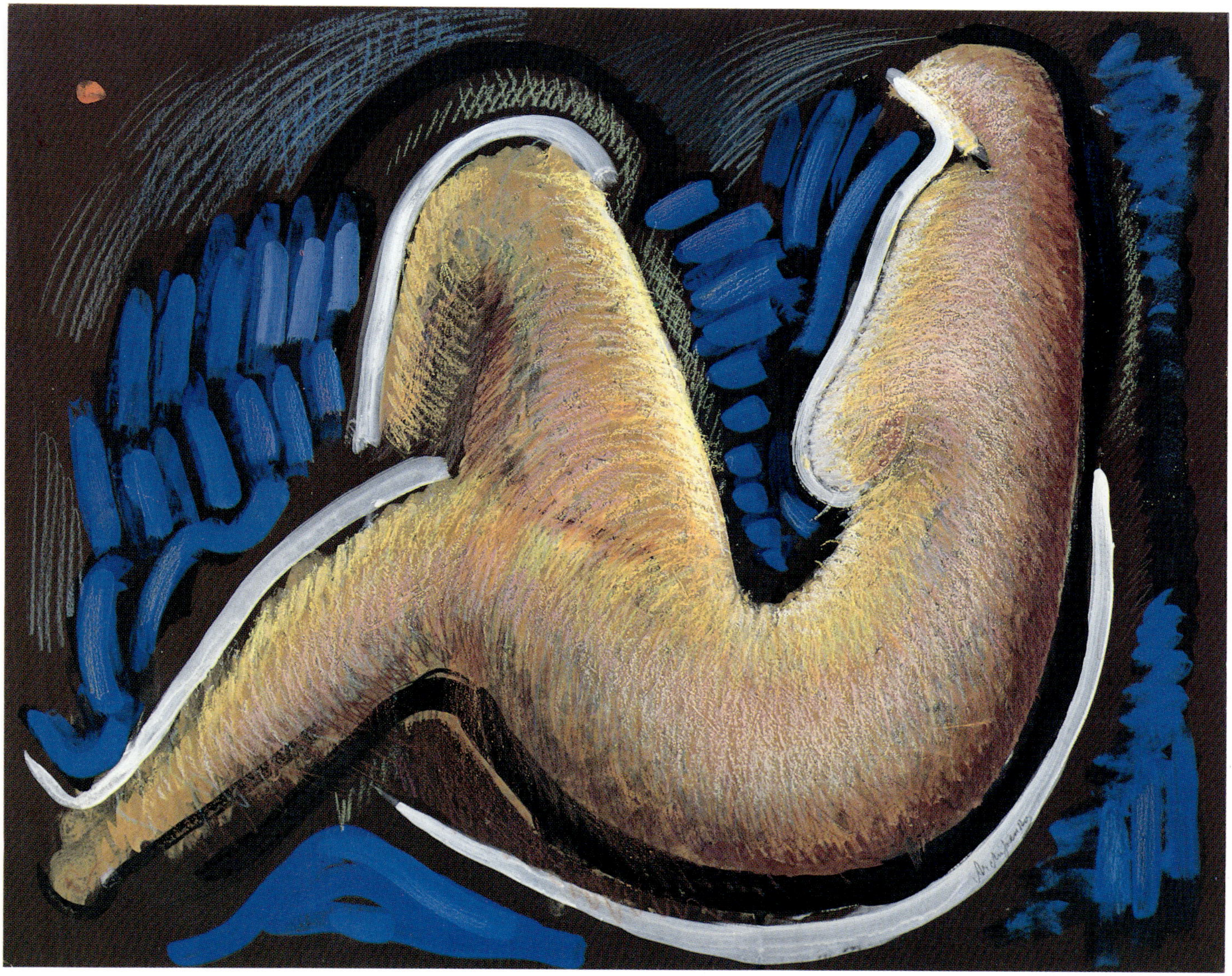

Alex Casler

II-7
FIGURE, 1960
Colored pencil and tempera
28×22″
Collection: Frances Archipenko Gray

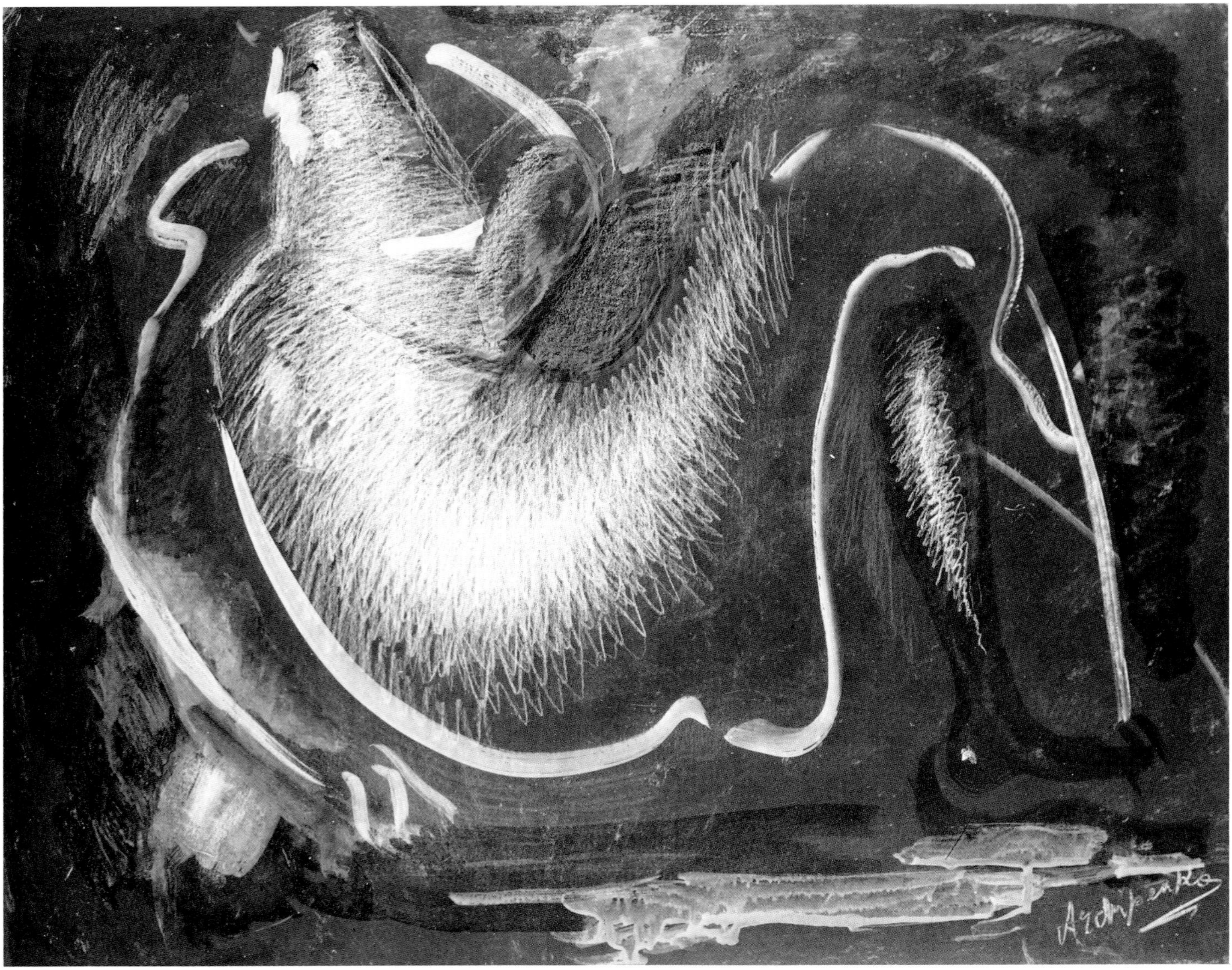

Alex Casler

Here Archipenko's characteristic construction of a figure from distinct, biomorphic segments is coupled with the gestural yet controlled brushstroke of his later works to produce a simple, delicate figure in repose. Works which relate to this watercolor include *Reclining Figure*, a gouache and pencil of 1949 in which the forms are much more tightly structured, and *Kneeling*, a watercolor of 1960 which displays a similar color scheme and even looser brushwork.[21]

II-8

RECLINING FIGURE, (REPOSE), 1960

Watercolor and ink

8½ × 11″

Collection: Frances Archipenko Gray

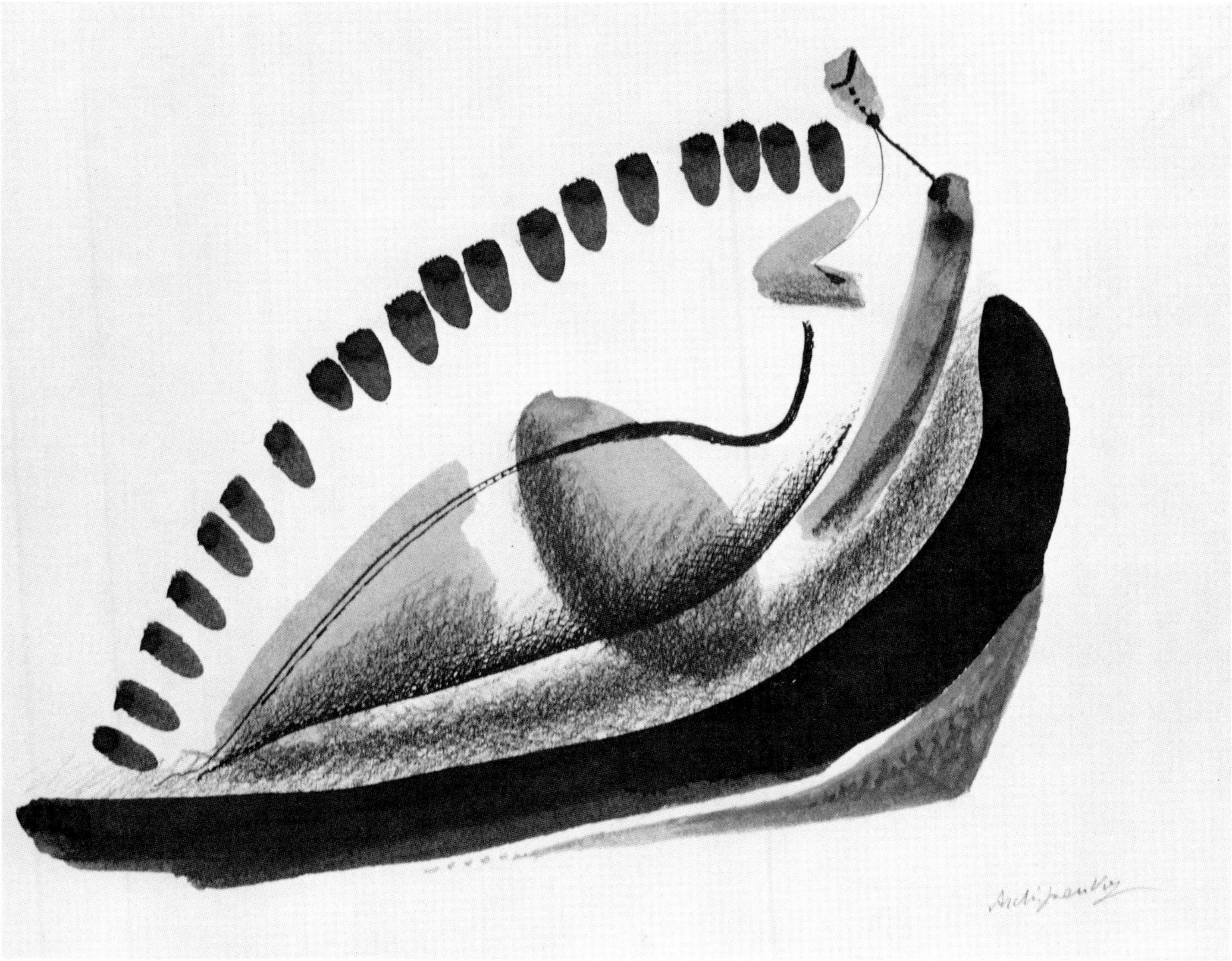

Alex Casler

II-9
RECLINING FIGURE, 1950s
Pencil
15 × 22″
Collection: Frances Archipenko Gray

These two unsigned and undated pieces (Plates II-9, II-10) bear a certain resemblance to figure types which Archipenko drew in the late 1930s. Their ill-defined anatomies, facelessness, and surrounding cross-hatched shadows are shared by works such as *Kneeling* and *Woman*, both of 1937.[22] The later date ascribed to the *Reclining Figures*, however, is based on their sketchy, hurried lines and loose renderings of form, traits not shared by the tightly structured and firmly delineated works of the 1930s.

Alex Casler

II-10
RECLINING FIGURE, 1950s
Pencil
15 × 22″
Collection: Frances Archipenko Gray

Alex Casler

III. STILL LIFE

III-1

STILL LIFE WITH VASE, 1921

Lithography

$17\frac{1}{8} \times 9\frac{1}{2}$"

Edition of 60

from the portfolio

Verlag Ernst Wasmuth, Berlin

Collection: Frances Archipenko Gray

During the late teens and early 1920s, Archipenko created a large number of typical Cubist still lifes in many media: lithography, pen and ink, watercolor, oil on canvas, and sculpto-paintings. These works are variations on a single theme, for they all partake of, in different selections and arrangements, the same set of deconstructed objects. The 1921 *Still Life with Vase* displays the three elements which all of Archipenko's still life compositions share: a centralized jug or vessel, a precariously tilted wooden table with lathe-worked legs, and patterns of checks or spots which may represent tablecloths or tiles, depending on their placement.

III-3
OBJECTS ON THE TABLE, 1957
Painted wood relief
25 × 17″
Collection: Frances Archipenko Gray

Late in his career, Archipenko began to cast images from his sculpto-painting in polychrome bronze versions. These two still lifes represent his first attempt at this translation from one relief medium to another. Although the two pieces contain the same number and arrangement of objects, subtle differences exist between them. Color plays a larger role in the sculpto-painting, helping to define three-dimensional forms and to create rich surface patterns, especially in the accentuated wood grain. The bronze piece displays fewer surface effects. The individual objects are more simple, and seem more organically related to one another. Thus, Archipenko used the specific properties of two distinct media to make separate formal statements from essentially identical images.

These reliefs are related to the artist's still lifes of c.1920, for they include the same central vessel and pitched wooden table, (see Plate III-1). The objects in the later pieces, however, are flattened, more abstracted, and rendered with a greater emphasis on curving contours.

III-4
OBJECTS ON TABLE, 1957
Bronze
25 × 17″
Collection: Frances Archipenko Gray

III-5
STILL LIFE WITH BOOK AND VASE ON TABLE, c.1960 (1918)
Bronze
18 × 13¾″
Collection: Frances Archipenko Gray

This bronze relief was also originally conceived as a sculpto-painting. Its forerunner, now lost, was a painted papier-mâché on wood relief contructed in 1918.[23] The arrangement of objects in the bronze, therefore, is typical of Archipenko's early still lifes. The piece deserves the date of its casting, however, because it is more an elaboration than a mere recreation of the image in the sculpto-painting. Archipenko rendered greater detail and surface texture in the later work, and that, coupled with the shift in medium, makes it a work of art closely related to, but independent of, the original piece.

IV. GROUP FIGURES AND FRAGMENTARY FIGURES

IV-1

REVELATION, 1952
Ink, gouache, gold leaf on canvas
36 × 18″
Collection: Frances Archipenko Gray

A single figure composed of a number of tightly knit, symmetrical forms, *Revelation* 's a composite of earlier sculptural motifs. Archipenko's famous *Vase Women*, free-standing sculptures begun in 1918, are the source for the figure's slim, columnar interior and spreading, arm-like projections.[24] The curved, encompassing exterior and nesting of forms can be seen in *Nun*, (sometimes called *Religious Figure*), a translucent lucite sculpture of 1948.[25] Together, these features form a female being of almost mythic presence who hovers before a gold ground. Archipenko's drawings of the 1950s increasingly included figures on gold, and of them he wrote, "Those on golden background achieve their effectiveness by the contrast of the materials and have a noble aspect, similar to a Persian painting or Byzantine ikon."[26]

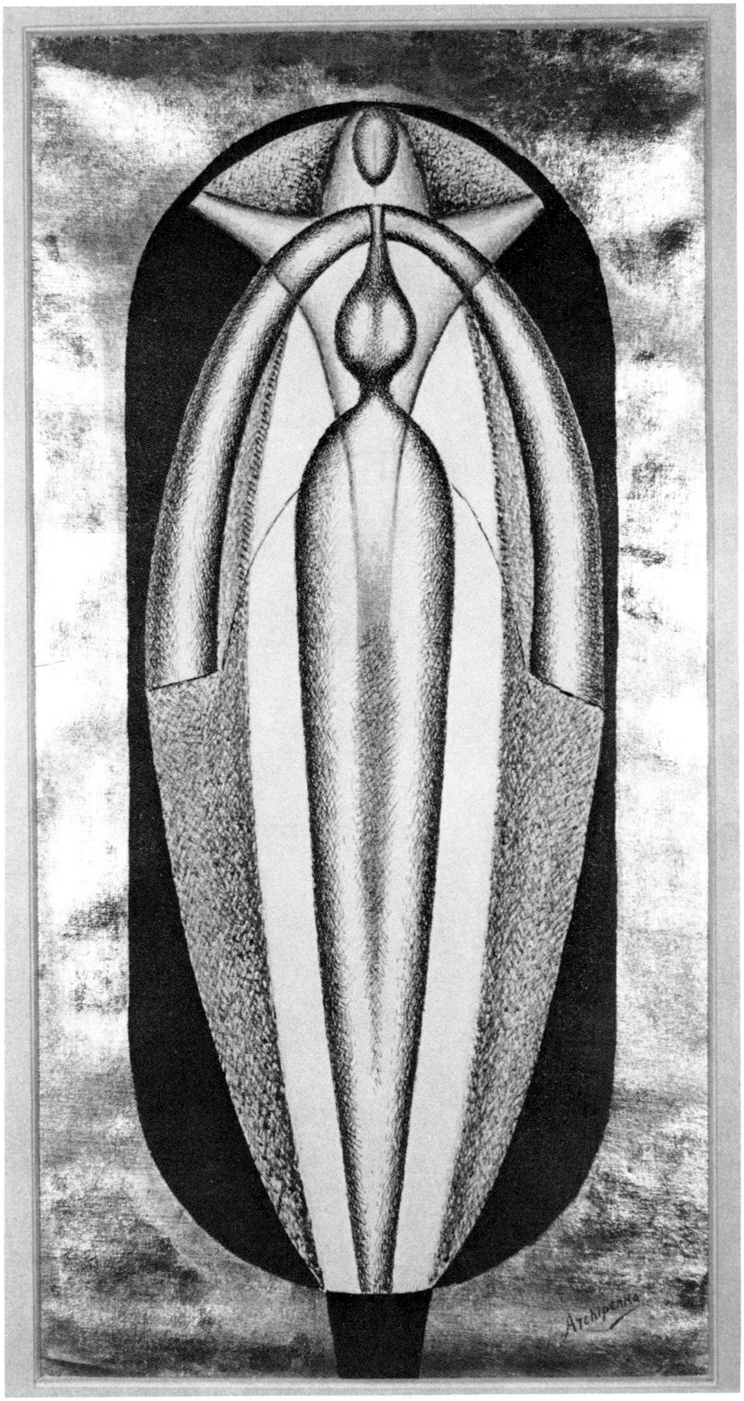

IV-3

TWO FIGURES (MEDIEVAL), 1954

Gouache

33×27″

Collection: Frances Archipenko Gray

Alex Casler

The gouache *Two Figures* is based on *Medieval*, a bronze polychrome relief cast in 1953.[27] Its dotted surface stems from the rough and pitted surface of the bronze work, and creates a shimmering field which seems to dissolve the two already fragmented bodies.

IV-4

ORANGE AND BLACK, 1957

Wood, metal, bakelite

24×48″

Collection: Frances Archipenko Gray

Created for his 1957 Perls Galleries show, the four sculpto-paintings that follow present images which are a far cry from those which appeared in Archipenko's original Cubist versions. One of the two qualities shared by the two sets of works is the fragmentation of the human figure, providing that one wishes to regard the later pieces as containing anthropomorphic references. The tripartite biomorph in *Orange and Black* becomes a female figure only when viewed in the context of Archipenko's earlier reliefs; it is then revealed to be a reduced, stylized descendant of works such as the *Metal Lady* (Plate I-4), and *Venus* (Plate I-7). *Red* includes vague allusions of human structures—a severely distorted mouth, squat legs, shadowy ears, and an elongated nose which partially obscures a Cyclopean eye—but the "figure" is so unlike anything ever created by the artist that its identity remains unclear. *Oval Figure* is hardly a figure at all. It seems rather to indicate the absence of a figure, a figure which has shattered and broken away from its enclosing, constraining exoskeleton. *White* is the most anthropoid being of this group, with a definable head, torso, and arm. This figure is still at a great remove from Archipenko's erotic renderings of women forty years earlier. It is a cold, blank-eyed, almost sinister plastic robot.

Another feature common to these reliefs, in addition to their dubious or strained humanity, is the substance bakelite. Bakelite is a trade name for a pressure-cast plastic compound used in the manufacture of telephone receivers, molded plastic ware, electric insulators, and other industrial and consumer products. It has a smooth surface of uniform color, and can be cast into any shape imaginable, which made it a popular material for furniture and decorative items in 1950s interior design schemes. Archipenko's use of bakelite, coupled with the bright colors and pattern effects in his sculpto-paintings, has caused some writers to link his late work to prevailing tastes in industrial and decorative arts.[28]

IV-5
RED, 1957
Wood, bakelite
48×36″
Collection: Frances Archipenko Gray

IV-6

OVAL FIGURE, 1957

Wood, metal, bakelite

43 × 36½″

Collection: Frances Archipenko Gray

IV-7
WHITE, 1957
Wood, bakelite
37 × 43″
Collection: Frances Archipenko Gray

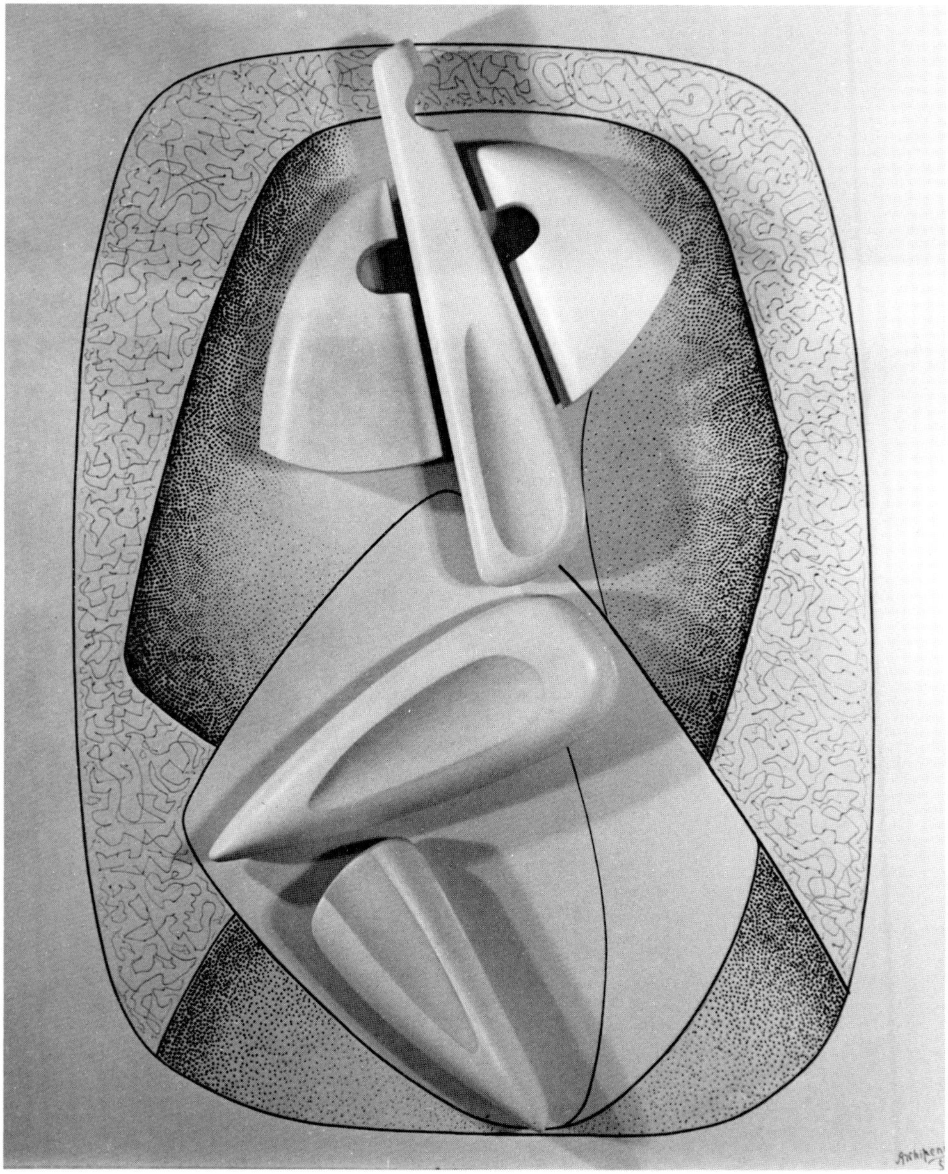

IV-8

CONVERSATION, 1959

Bronze on marble

27 × 14½″

Collection: Frances Archipenko Gray

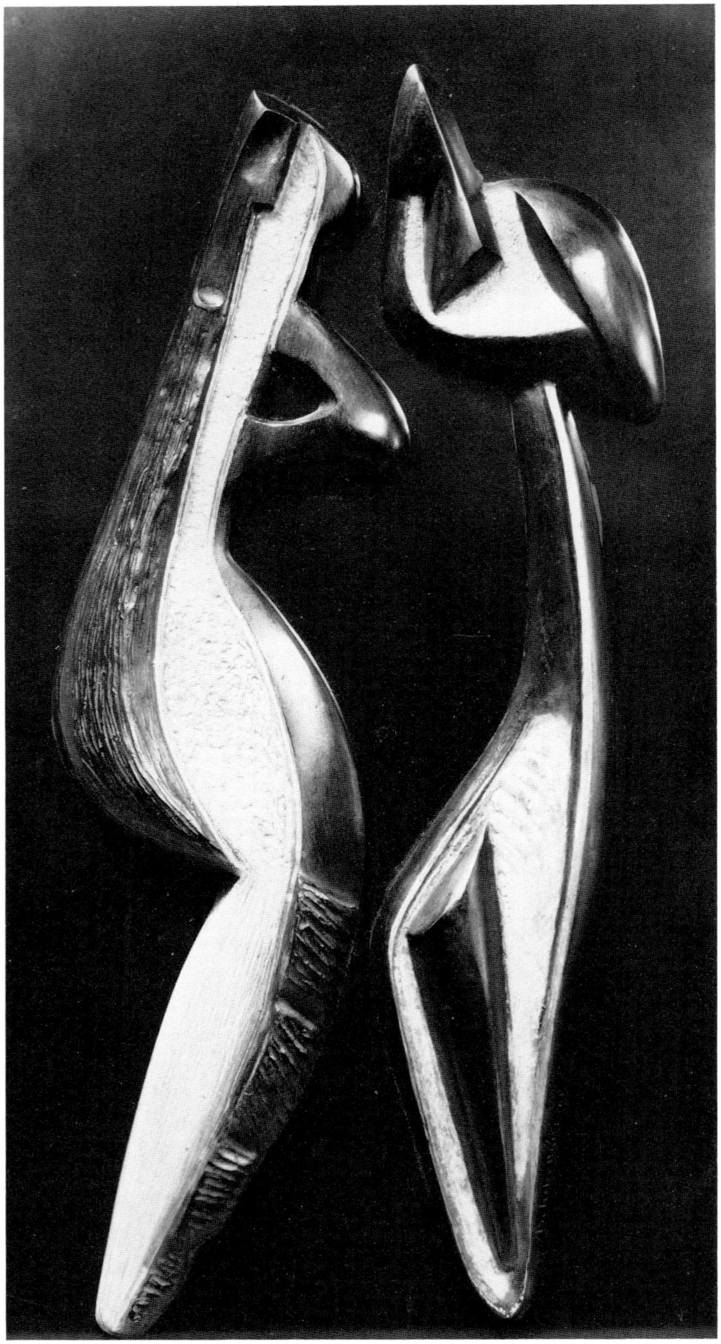

Some writers have criticized these bronze on marble pieces for having an exclusive emphasis on materials.[29] This, however, is too facile a reading. Something more complex is revealed when these closely-related works, all created for a one-man show of bronzes at the Perls Gallery in 1959, are analyzed as a series. *Conversation* depicts two highly abstracted, interacting human figures, akin to earlier pairings such as in the lithograph *Two Figures* (cat. IV-2). In the bronze *Two Figures*, the bodies are pulled apart into biomorphic segments which are held loosely together by firmly delineated amoebic forms. The figures in *Fragmentary Relief* exhibit a further deconstruction: bodily integrity is destroyed, and the forms oscillate between individuality and gestalt groupings. In *Eagle* no figures remain, only vaguely aquatic biomorphs which resemble mounted fossils.

This devolution from the human to the primeval illustrates a universal continuum of life and matter. Archipenko firmly believed in such a cosmic structural underpinning. His later writings continually allude to formal and spiritual constants of being, with statements such as: "Universal dynamism mingles planetary forces with those of our cells in a continual creative evolution. If consciousness will embrace this inevitableness, the individual will grasp the creative reality within nature as well as within himself and may express it in many forms."[30]

The materials past which Archipenko's critics could not see were chosen by the artist for philosophic as well as aesthetic purposes. Bronze and marble, inorganic metal and stone, are activated and transformed by their rich, earthy colors into primal living beings and forces, which then engage in a drama of combination and recombination, evolution and devolution, universal flux.

IV-9
TWO FIGURES, 1959
Bronze on marble
21 × 14½"
Collection: Frances Archipenko Gray

IV-10

FRAGMENTARY RELIEF, 1959

Bronze on marble

23 × 14″

Collection: Frances Archipenko Gray

IV-11
EAGLE, 1959
Bronze on marble
10½ × 15½"
Collection: Frances Archipenko Gray

IV-12

WOMAN WITH FAN, c.1958 (1914)

Bronze

35¾″ high

Collection: Frances Archipenko Gray

These pieces appeared in Archipenko's second show of bronzes at the Perls Gallery in 1962. Like the bronze *Still Life with Book and Vase on Table* (Plate III-5.), *Woman with Fan* and *Standing Woman* are both based on much earlier sculpto-paintings.[31] The original images are considerably reworked in the bronze versions. Certain planar forms are redisposed or eliminated entirely, and surface patterns and textures reflect the properties of their new medium. Works of art in their own right, these pieces bear the dates of their castings.

IV-13
STANDING WOMAN, c.1960 (1920)
Bronze
28½ × 16⅜″
Collection: Frances Archipenko Gray

IV-14

TWO FIGURES, 1960

Gouache and colored pencil

21½ × 27½"

Collection: Frances Archipenko Gray

The figures in this drawing are greatly abstracted, with notched heads similar to the ones which appear in the bronze and lithograph versions of *Standing Women* (Plate IV-13). Despite the formal reduction, the image is heavily laden with sexual overtones. The woman on the left is the picture of fecundity with her ripe, swelling breast, loins, and thigh, while the male figure is little more than a phallus. Swirling plasmic fields, as well as a leg which seems to be held in common, unite the figures in what appears to be an allegory of cosmic procreation.

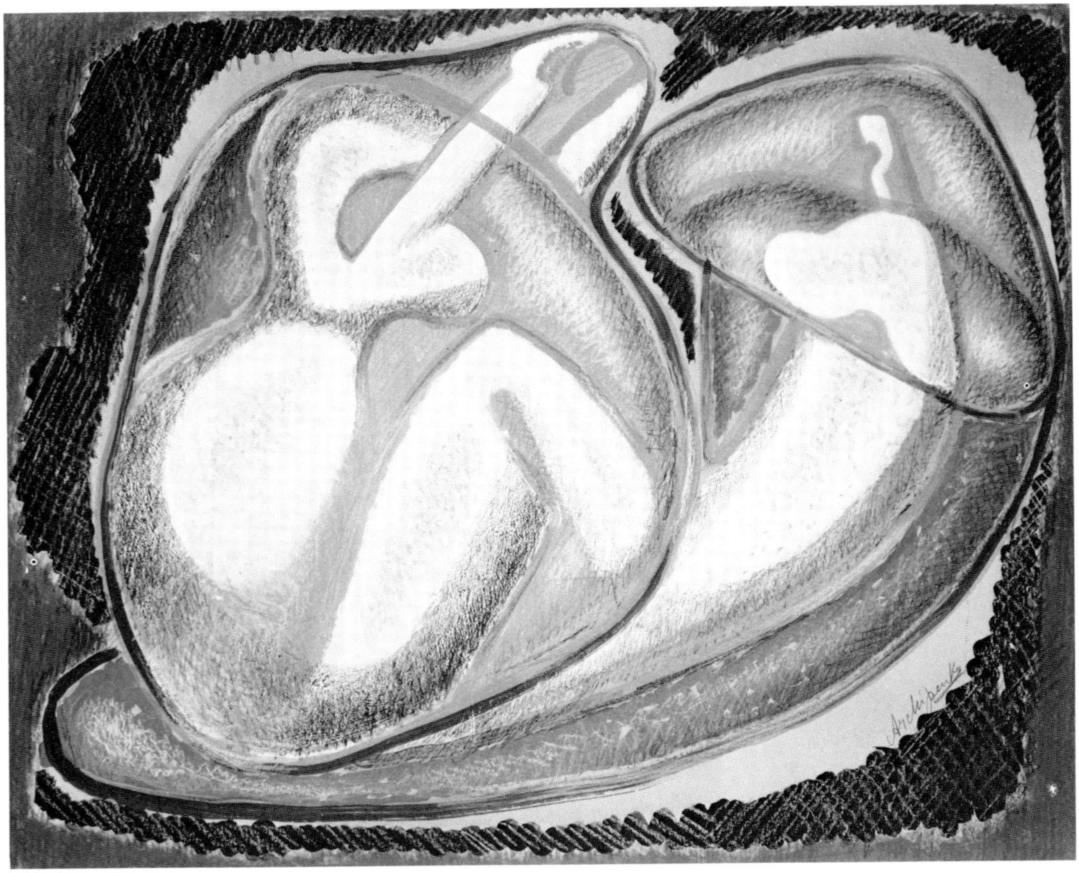

IV-15

TWO FIGURES, 1961

Gouache, colored pencil, pastel

$28\frac{2}{5} \times 22\frac{2}{5}''$

Collection: Frances Archipenko Gray

Alex Casler

Two monumental, radiant beings appear in this drawing. Their imposing presence is achieved through formal borrowings from the traditions of Byzantine and Slavic icon painting which Archipenko applied to his own multiple-biomorph figural idiom. The figures are linear, static, and flat, and dominate the picture plane by their sheer size. Rendered with glowing colors, they float on or before a contrasting, nebulous ground. To the right of the composition, a figure reminiscent of the ethereal being in *Revelation* (Plate IV-1) is shown frontally. The figure to its left, constructed of overlapping and intertwined biomorphs (as in Plates I-7, I-10, II-5, IV-4, etc.), faces right in an attitude of homage or obeisance. This gesture amplifies the calm stateliness of the picture.

IV-16

PROPHET AND WOMAN, 1961

Gouache, pastel

26½ × 21¼″

Collection: Frances Archipenko Gray

Prophet and Woman is a bridge piece between *Two Figures* (Plate IV-15), and the *Herodias and Salome* works (Plates IV-17, IV-18). Its left-hand figure appears in the former, and its right-hand figure is a simple version of the gyrating dancers in the latter. The rough, informal quality of the drawing may indicate that it served as the original sketch for the two figure types.

Alex Casler

IV-17

HERODIAS AND SALOME, 1962

Lithograph

25¼ × 19¼″

Edition of 20

Collection of Frances Archipenko Gray, New York

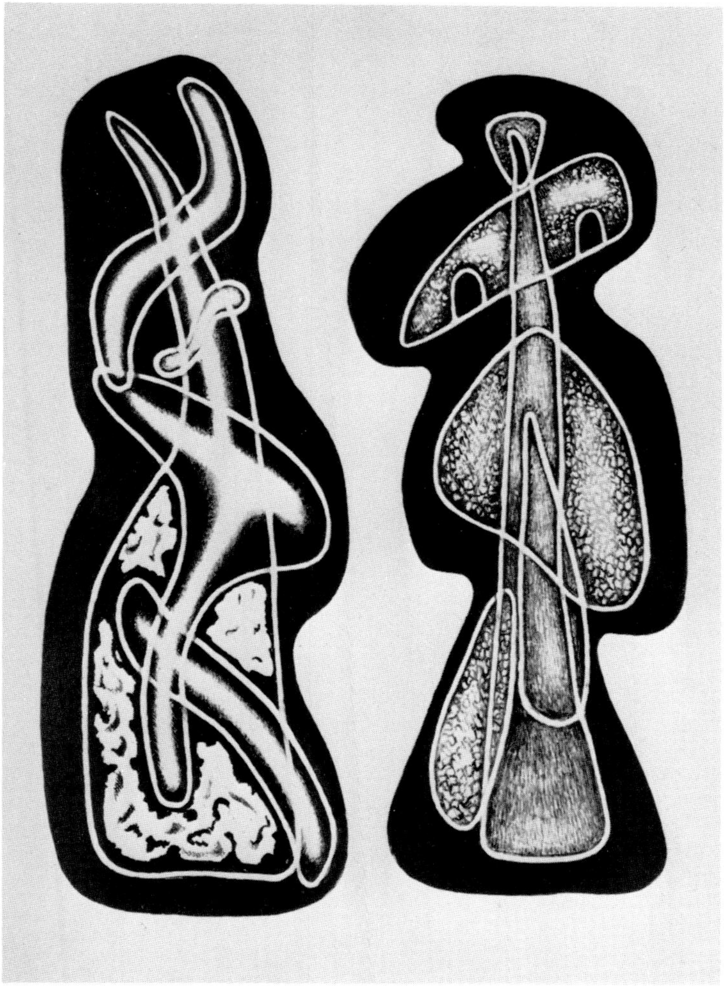

Iconic figures composed of multiple biomorphs appear again in these two works, as well as a new dimension: specific narrative content. Archipenko used his characteristically ambiguous forms to illustrate an event from the New Testament, Salome's dance. The imposing Herodias, King Herod's illegitimate wife, stands on the left, watching her daughter and co-conspirator Salome dance for the head of John the Baptist.[32]

Archipenko's skill as a printmaker is evidenced by the lithograph, wherein stark contrasts of black and white assume the emotive function of the bright colors in the drawing.

IV-18

TWO FIGURES, 1961

Gouache and colored pencil

$28\frac{2}{5} \times 22\frac{2}{5}$"

Collection: Frances Archipenko Gray

Alex Casler

IV-19
THREE FIGURES, 1962
Gouache
12×14½″
Collection: Frances Archipenko Gray

This colorful gouache is based on an ink drawing of 1960 which bears the same title.[33] In the earlier piece, the figures are flat, defined by loose, gestural applications of ink. The gouache is a more finished piece. Body components are modelled, a multi-colored patterned field replaces cross-hatched shadows, and the composition is structured with a tight linearity.

IV-20

THREE FRAGMENTARY FIGURES, 1962

(Fluctuating Figures)

Collage, chalk

28½ × 22″

Collection: Frances Archipenko Gray

Ambiguity of form is a major theme of this work. Here Archipenko employed a number of devices to create fluctuations between figure and ground, mass and void. The three figures, although of great size, are really quiet insubstantial. They float rather than rest upon their rectangular platform, and they seem to be translucent. Invdividual forms are modelled in a strange and cursory fashion, leaving the viewer unsure of their intended spatial dimension. Certain voids are given the quality of mass, and Archipenko's familiar cross-hatched ectoplasm appears as either a solid or a misty gas, depending upon its placement. The dark, central diagonal element further complicates the picture. More opaque than the other forms, it is placed behind the figures to register varying degrees of inconsistent transparency.

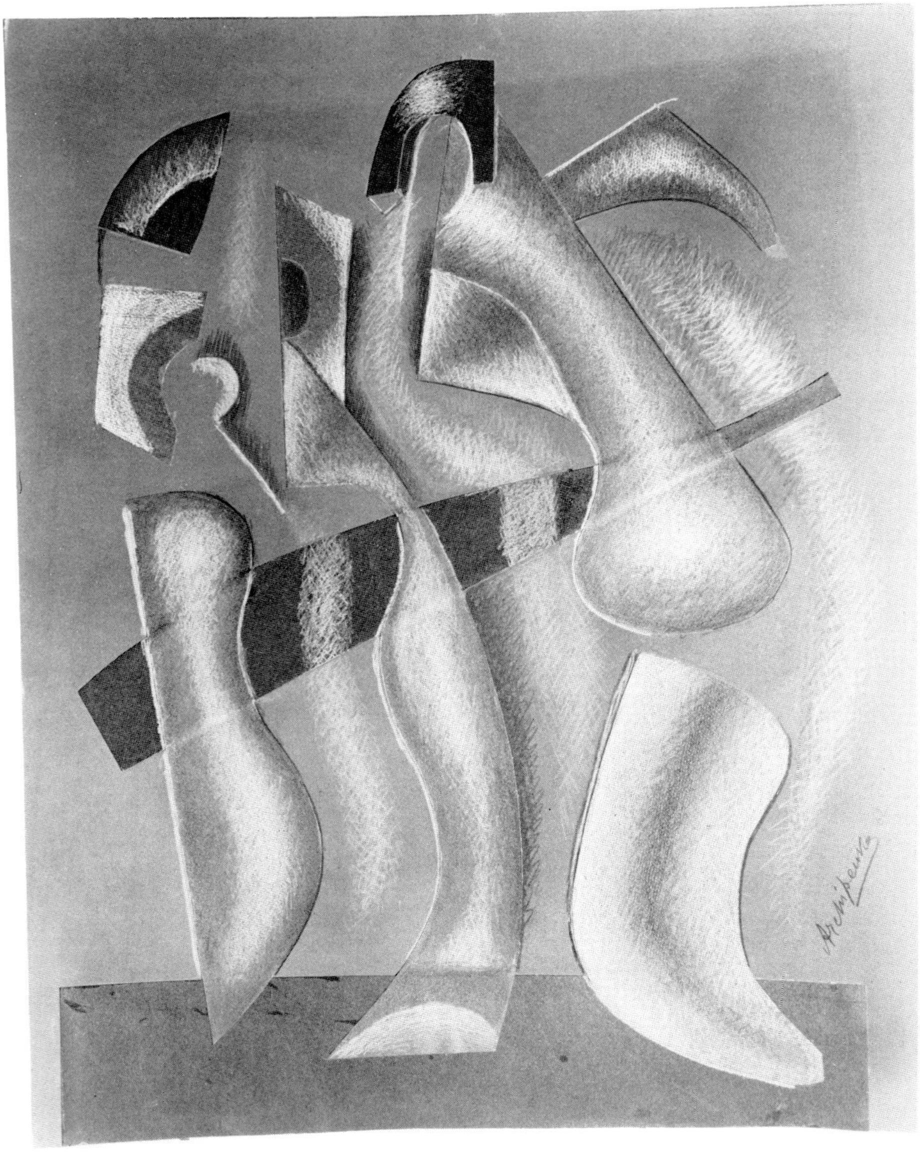

IV-21
SEATED AND STANDING FIGURES, 1962
Lithograph
23¼ × 17¼″
Collection: Frances Archipenko Gray

Archipenko's mastery of form/void relationships is clearly evident in this lithograph. He plays against one another the polar opposites of black and white, and uses each to create both substance and emptiness. Despite the ambiguity of individual forms, they mesh together to constitute five fragmentary but easily readable figures. This formal exercise is not an end in itself, however, for the scene enacted by the five bizarre beings is one of high drama, with overlays of complex emotional content and associations.

IV-22
ENCOUNTER, 1963
Lithograph
19¾ × 10⅞"
Edition of 50
Collection: Frances Archipenko Gray

These two conversers derive from similar pairings in Archipenko's *oeuvre,* such as the bronze *Conversation* (Plate IV-8), and the lithograph *Two Figures* (cat. IV-2). *Encounter* presents the liveliest image, yet is rendered with the greatest economy of form.

IV-23

LIVING FORMS (LES FORMES VIVANTES), 1962-1963

Lithographs

Edition of 75

From the portfolio *Les formes vivantes,* Erker-presse, St. Gallen, Switzerland, 1963

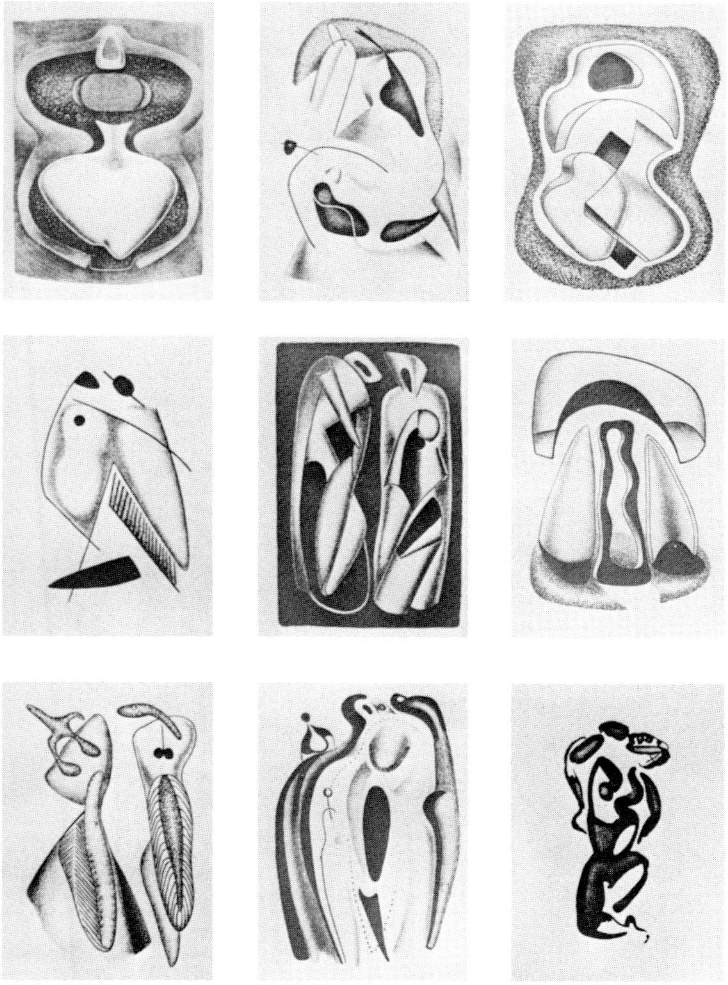

This series of ten lithographs was finished by Archipenko in the winter of 1963, a year before his death. They were the last prints of his career and stand as a milestone in his *oeuvre.* Intended as images to be later worked into sculptures, (an unrealized project), the prints also sum up many of his artistic accomplishments.[34] Pictured is a group of nine of the lithographs from the original portfolio. On the following pages we are reproducing eight of the lithographs individually. Not shown individually are nos. IV-23.8, *The Luminosity of Forms,* and IV-23.10, *Rendezvous of Four Forms.*

IV-23.1

THE LOVERS

22¾ × 14¾"

The Lovers unifies two themes found throughout Archipenko's work: eroticism and communication between two figures. This piece blends the sexual coupling of *Two Figures* (Plate IV-14) with the abstracted, conversing bodies of *Encounter* (Plate IV-22) to create a gentle image of spiritual and physical love.

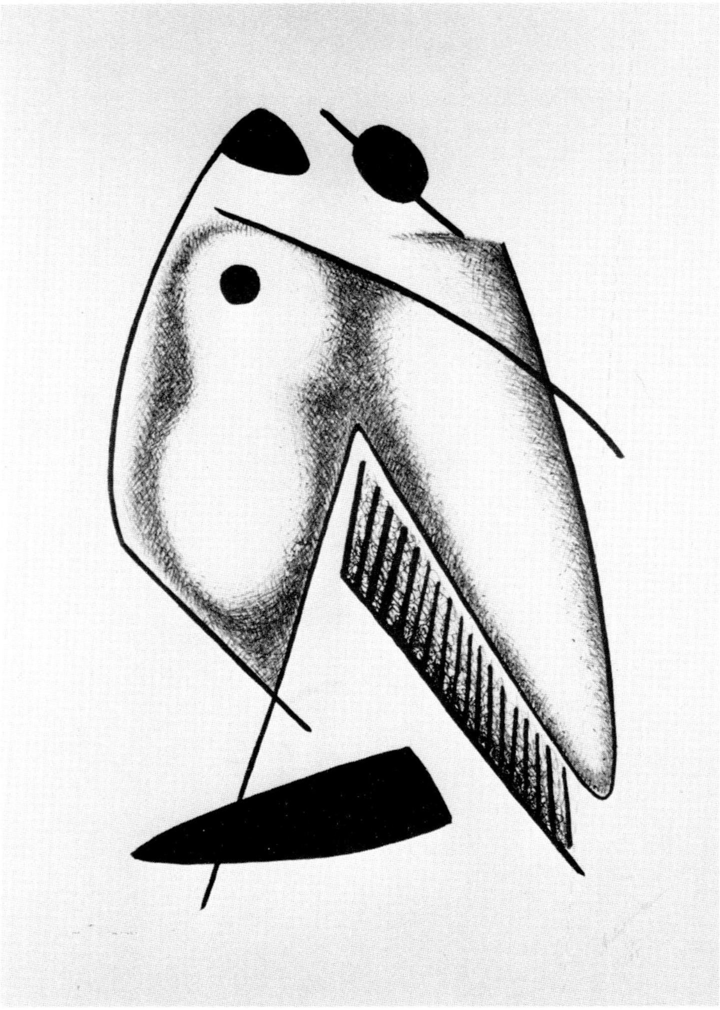

IV-23.2
BLACK DANCE
21½ × 10¼″

Of all the prints in this series, this is the only one which takes as its model a work from Archipenko's early career. It is based on a 1924 wash drawing, and is imbued with the gestural fluidity of many of the artist's late drawings and watercolors.

IV-23.3

THE GROUP

26 × 17½″

The simple biomorphs and lack of coherent identifiable figures in this lithograph indicate that it relates to Archipenko's images of deconstructed physical laws and organic processes, such as the bronzes *Fragmentary Relief* and *Eagle* (Plates IV-10, and IV-11).

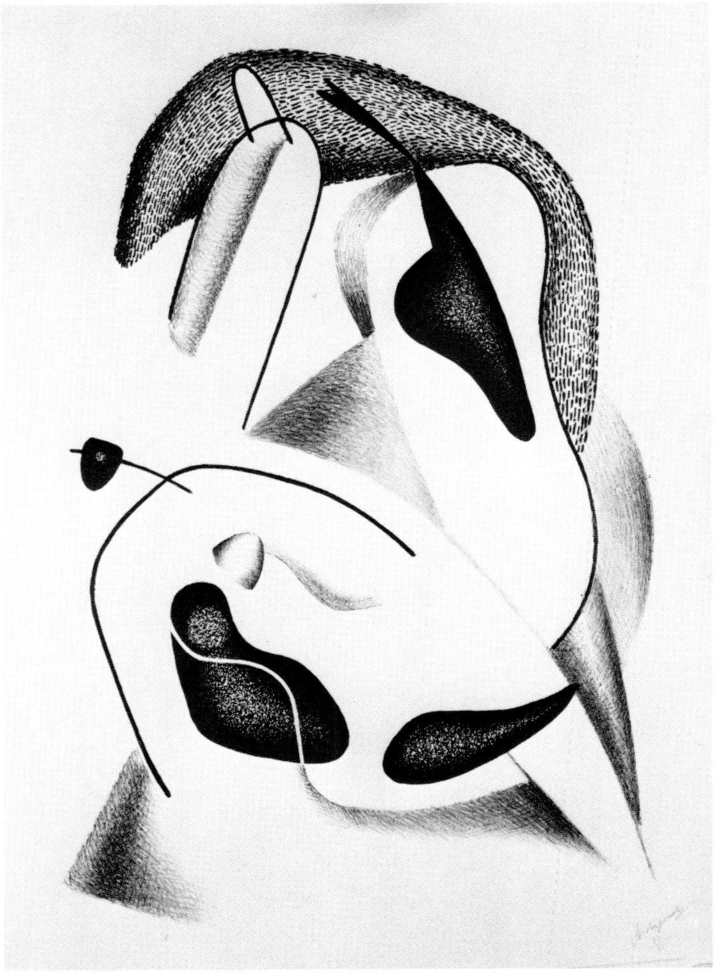

IV-23.4

THE MANNIKINS

25½ × 15¾″

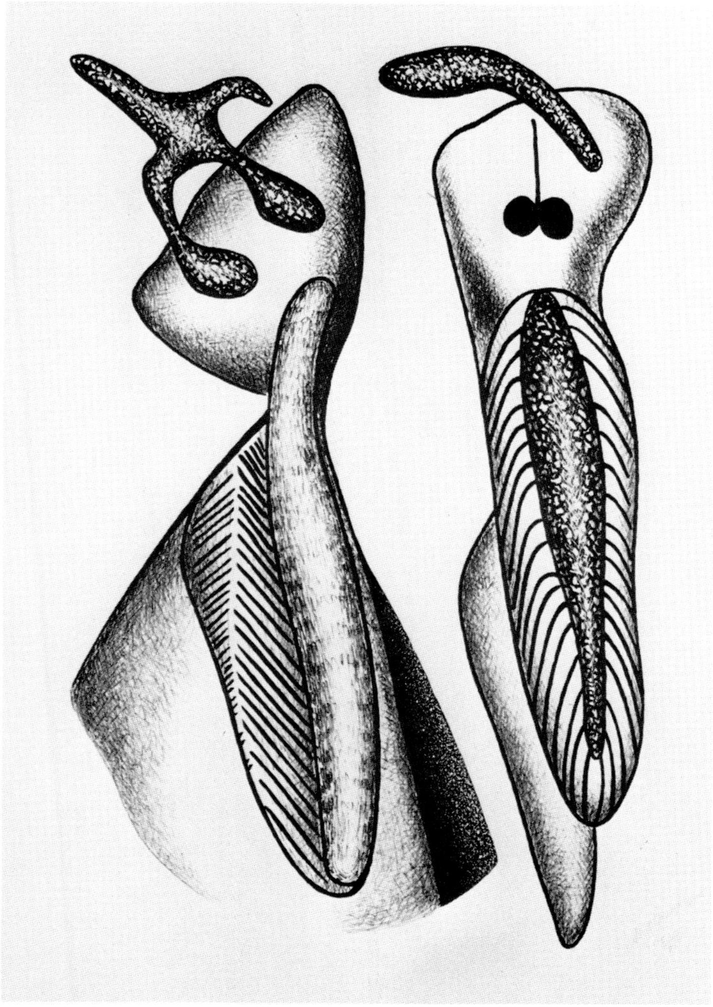

The last in a long line of assembled biomorphs, *The Mannikins* also displays the iconic features developed by Archipenko in his late colored drawings. (see Plates IV-15, and IV-18.)

IV-23.5

THE FAMILY OF ONE FORM

26¼ × 18″

Another example of Archipenko's virtuoso handling of positive and negative spaces and shapes, this print is close kin to *Seated and Standing Figures* (Plate IV-21). In this piece, however, forms and voids are manipulated to obscure the exact number and specific identities of the figures. Thus the group takes prominence over the individual. *The Family of One Form* is an exploration of the concept of family, not a simple enumeration or portrait of family members.

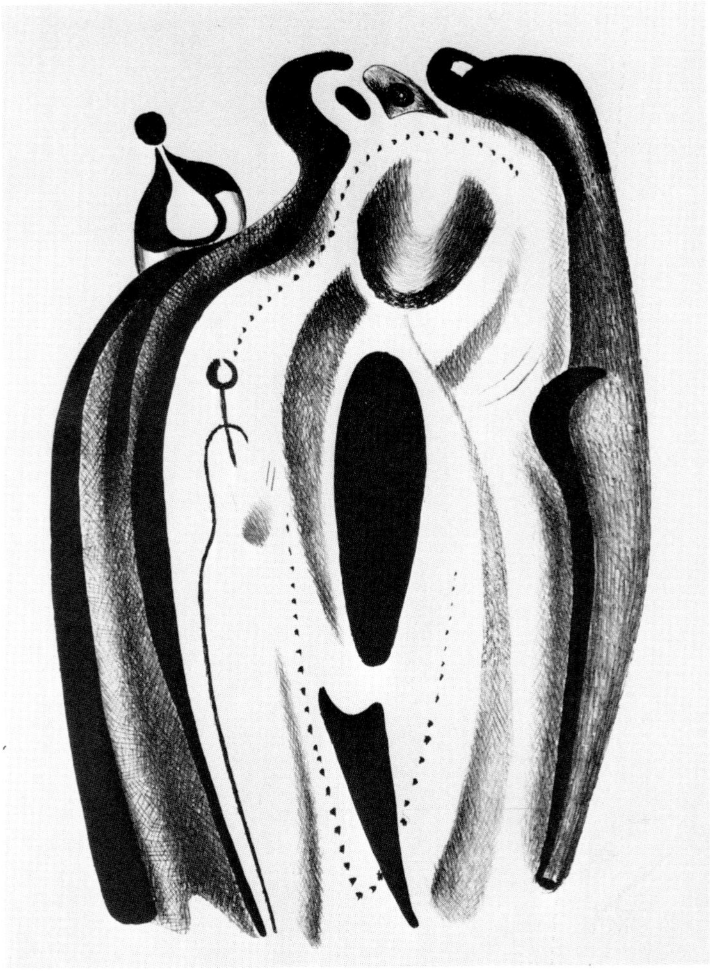

IV-23.6

CORONATION OF FORMS

25 × 17½″

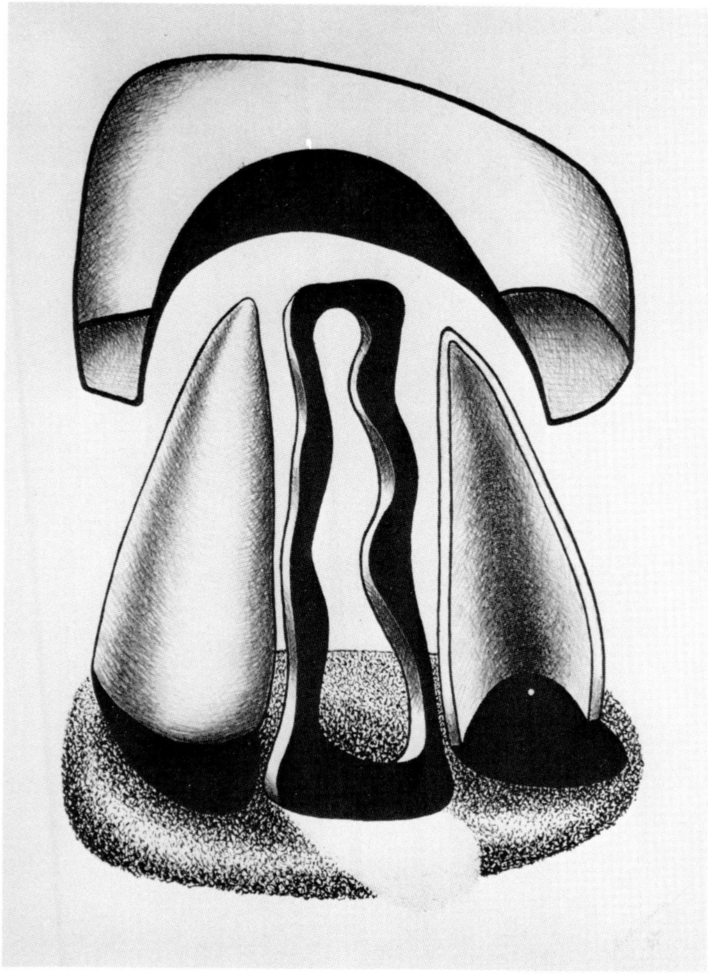

In this lithograph Archipenko crowns, or makes a triumphal arch of, his own crowning achievement: the manipulation of convex, concave, and void forms which has guaranteed him a prominent position in the history of modern sculpture. The artist used these forms not only as aesthetic devices, but also as signifiers for psychological and natural constants. In 1960 he wrote, "We cannot deny that in our psychological make-up the positive and the negative are of identical force and we merely apply them in different proportions according to our orientation and interest in a particular case. In our daily lives our 'yes' and 'no' are both centered around the same point of interest and used as positive or negative decisions according to our personal advantage. All positive and negative by the nature of polarity become one. . . . In the creative process, as in life itself, the reality of the negative is a conceptual imprint of the absent positive. . . . It is not exactly the presence of a thing but rather the absence of it that becomes the cause and impulse for creative motivation. This process exists in nature as a latent force and is the fundamental creative inducer of new organic life. Nature creates that which is not yet there. The apprehension and use of this principle by an individual may guide him to the understanding of many transcendental values of art and life."[35]

IV-23.7a

ENCIRCLED FORMS

17×27½"

A reclining and fragmentary figure is created by interlocking, overlapping, and juxtaposed forms in this print. The forms, in turn, are defined entirely by looping white lines. Distinct lines were important elements in Archipenko's work: lines defined by sculptural form in his three-dimensional objects, and line defining form in his two-dimensional pieces. "In spite of the general difference in conception," Archipenko wrote, "all my drawings are united by their characteristic purity of line which is derived from my (sculptural) style."[36]

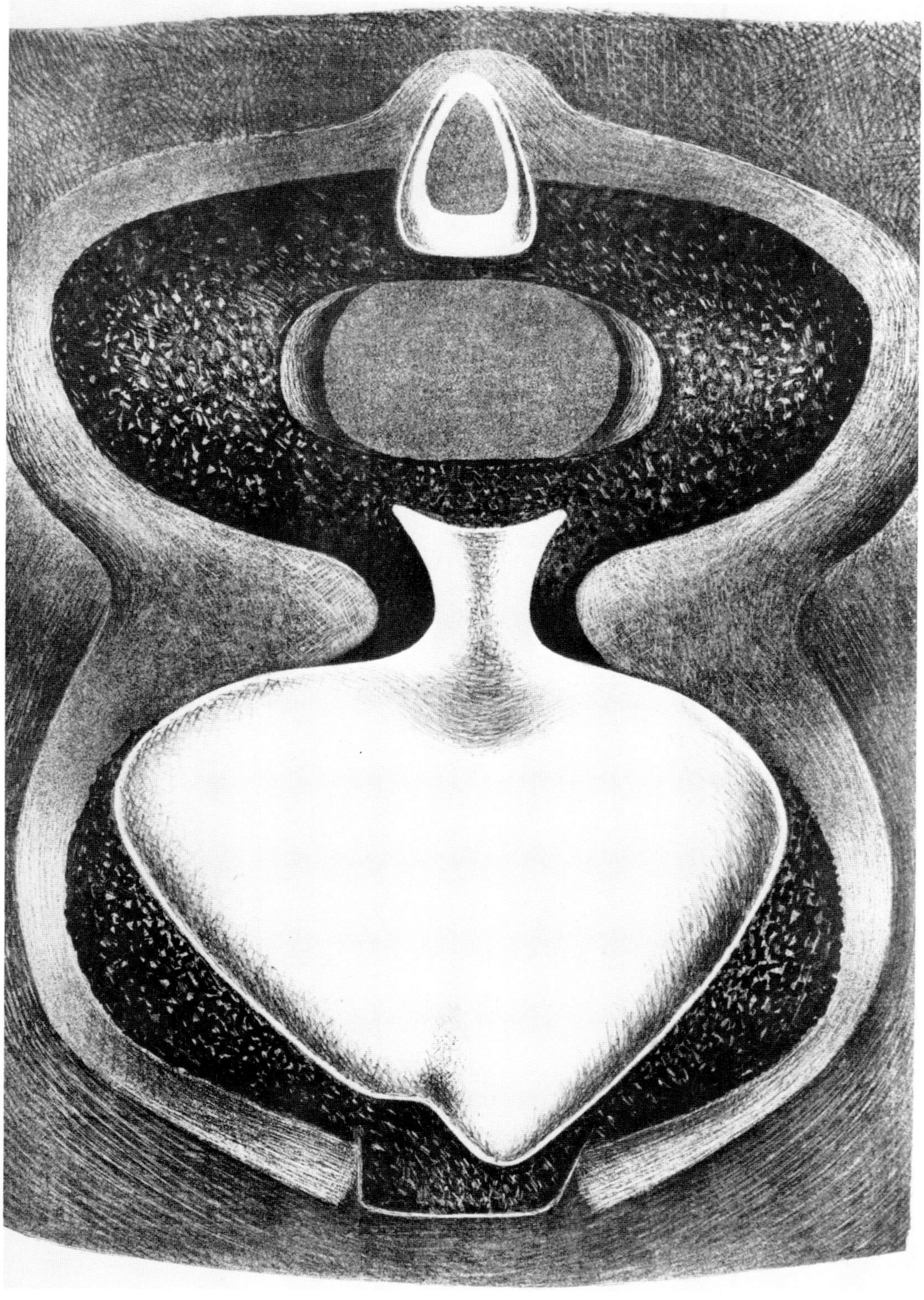

IV-23.9a

MAJESTIC FORMS

25¾ × 18⅝″

The lithograph *Majestic Forms* departs from its original drawing by the elimination of the lower leg forms and the elongation of the central lacuna. This prominent hole relates the work to Archipenko's early pioneering sculptures, and its frontality and imposing presence indicate that it descends from his iconic figures of the 1950s and 1960s (see Plates IV-1, IV-15, IV-17, and IV-18).

V. OTHER WORKS

V-1.

THE MOON, 1947
Carved plastic, electric light
12 × 12½"
Collection of Frances Archipenko Gray, New York

The Moon is an anomaly in Archipenko's *oeuvre,* for it represents neither a human figure nor an organic form. One can understand the artist's interest in the subject, however, for the moon is a work of nature, it is filled with and creates mystery, and is a luminous body.

Archipenko included transparent materials in his sculpture as early as 1912. His construction *Medrano I* (Fig. 2) contained a piece of glass. During the year 1946, he began to experiment with transparency on a much larger scale, fashioning free-standing figures of lucite and plexiglass. In 1947 he placed amber-colored electric light bulbs within translucent sculptures, thus illuminating them from within. *The Moon* is one of these works, and was first exhibited at the Associated American Artists Gallery in New York in 1948. For the exhibit's catalogue, Archipenko wrote: "Following my way of inventions in sculpture, I now use the conductivity of light in plastic. This success in modelling light has come after much experimentation. The plastic works in this exhibition consist of four aesthetic elements—first, modellings of space; second, concave; third, transparency; and, as the fourth element, the modelling of light effected by electricity."[37]

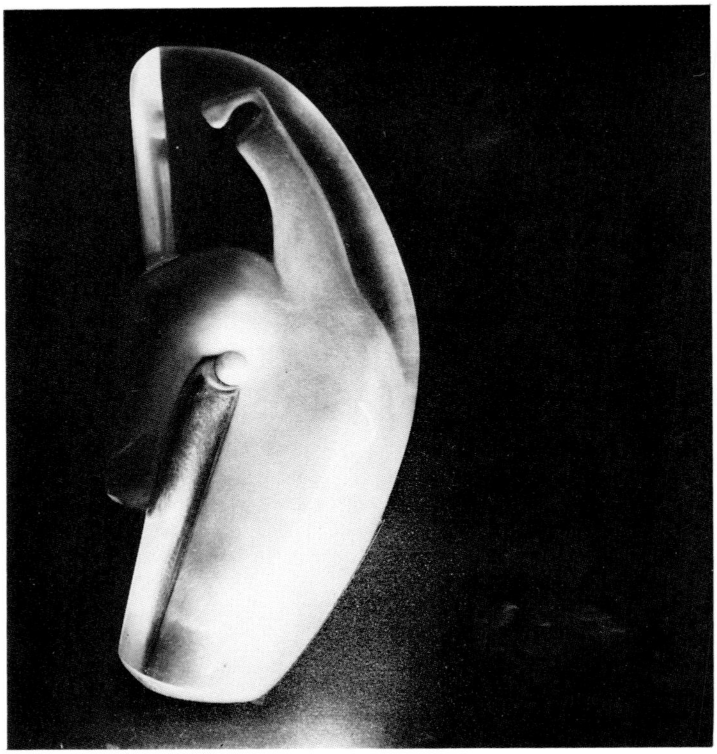

NOTES TO THE CATALOGUE

1 For the early history of Archipenko's sculpto-painting, see Michaelsen, 112-39.

2 Archipenko, 1960, 41.

3 For the "Woman with a Fan" theme in Cubism, see Taggard, 83-87.

4 For the 1914 *Woman with a Fan*, see Michaelsen, 129-30. Many of Archipenko's sculptures in Europe were destroyed by the Nazis during their purge of Modernism. His works were exhibited in Degenerate Art Exhibit in Munich in 1937. See Karshan, 1968, 42.

5 Karshan, 1975, 49.

6 For the Berlin lithographs, see *ibid.*, 76-101. The lithograph *Two Figures* (1920-1921) juxtaposes the two figural styles in one image.

7 Quoted in Little Gallery, 13.

8 Illustrated in Archipenko, 1960, pl. 13.

9 *Relief* was first exhibited at the Kunstmuseum Düsseldorf in 1960. See Wiese, 1960, cat. 36. Archipenko's 1954 retrospective was at the Associated American Artists Gallery in New York. See Associated American Artists, 1954, cat. 74, for a reproduction of *Plaster Relief*.

10 Quoted in Rzepecki, 16.

11 *Torso in Ceramic and Mosaic* is reproduced in Casson, pl. 19.

12 For *Woman in Front of a Mirror*, see Michaelsen, 122-23. The work was destroyed in Germany in 1921.

13 Archipenko, 1960, 59.

14 All of the sculpto-paintings created for the Perls Gallery show appear in this catalogue: Plates I-9, I-10, II-5, III-3, IV-4, IV-5, IV-6, and IV-7.

15 Reproduced in Archipenko, 1960, pl. 10.

16 For reproductions of the 1935 *Torsos in Space*, see *ibid.*, pl.s 185, 186.

17 For *Black Torso* and *White Torso*, see Michaelsen, cat. S48, cat. S70.

18 See Archipenko, 1960, 64-5.

19 Archipenko's *Medrano I* (fig. 2), of 1912, contained three found objects: two bails and a disc. This innovation predates Picasso's inclusion of a real spoon in his famous *Glass of Absinthe* of 1914, thus establishing Archipenko as the first modern artist to employ found objects. For the importance of *Medrano I*, see Karshan, 1975, 11-23.

20 The 1927 *Cleopatra* is illustrated in Bulliet, cat. 3.

21 *Reclining Figure* (1949) is reproduced in Archipenko, 1960, pl. 247. *Kneeling* is reproduced in Fuchs, cat. 46.

22 These drawings are reproduced in Karshan, 1968, 57, fig. 37, and fig. 38.

23 The sculpto-painting *Still Life with Book and Vase on Table* is reproduced and discussed in Michaelsen, 137, 198, cat. S89.

24 See Karshan, 1968, 35-38.

25 *Nun* is reproduced in Wiese, 1960, fig. 40.

26 From a typed statement by Archipenko, "Information of (sic) the Exhibited Drawings by Alexander Archipenko," which accompanied the catalogue to his 1950 drawing show at the Bowdoin College Museum of Fine Arts.

27 The bronze *Medieval* is reproduced in Wight, Kuh, and Karshan, 27, cat. 47.

28 See *ibid.*, 27; and Wasserman, 66. This popular taste element in 1950s sculpture may be more prevalent than previously suspected. In a recent article Carter Ratcliff claims that the braze-and-weld sculptures of Ibram Lassaw, Theodore Roszak, Seymour Lipton, David Hare, and Herbert Ferber, among others, "easily transposed to the decor of a mildly adventurous living room from the early 1950s." See Ratcliff, 145-48.

29 See A.J.M., 15; and Munsterberg, 55.

30 Archipenko, 1960, 17. See also his chapter on form, 31-38. Not surprisingly, the biomorphs in *Eagle* bear a certain resemblance to microscopic foraminifera illustrated on page 32.

31 For the sculpto-paintings *Woman with Fan* and *Standing Woman*, see Michaelsen, 129-30, 181, cat. S58; and 137, 209, cat. S112.

32 This story is related in Matt. 14:1-12, and Mark 6:16-29, King James Version.

33 The ink drawing *Three Figures* is reproduced in Fuchs, cat. 50.

34 Karshan, 1975, 57-59, gives a detailed account of the printing of the portfolio.

35 Archipenko, 1960, 53-54.

36 See note 26.

37 Quoted in Associated American Artists, 1948.

CHECKLIST OF THE EXHIBITION

by Nicholas J. Capasso

I. STANDING FIGURES

I-1. **BATHER,** 1915
Oil and pencil on metal, wood, and paper
20 × 11½″
Philadelphia Museum of Art, Louise and Walter Arensberg Collection

Bibliography: Archipenko, 1960, pl. 40, (illus. only); Barr, 103, 107, pl. 95, (illus.); Däubler and Goll, fig. 28, (illus. only); Elsen, 71 cat. 200, (illus.); Goll, 8, (illus. only); Hammacher, 139, 141, (illus.); Janis and Blesh, 115-16, (illus.); Lieberman and Kuh, cat. 14, (illus. only); Michaelsen, 127-8, 131-2, 183-4, cat. S62, (illus.); Philadelphia Museum of Art, cat. 1, (illus. only); Raynal, pl. 24, (illus. only); Rowell, cat. 27, (illus. only).

I-2. **WOMAN WITH FAN II,** 1915
Painted wood relief
19½ × 15¾″
Hirshhorn Museum and Sculpture Garden, Washington, D.C.

Bibliography: Courthion, 28, (illus.), 31; Lerner, 252, 359, pl. 348, (illus.); Michaelsen, 130-31, 184, cat. 564, (illus.); Roberts, 702, 704, fig. 122 (illus.).

I-4. **WOMAN (METAL LADY),** 1923
Brass, copper, wood, and new silver
54½ × 20½″
Yale University Art Gallery, New Haven

Bibliography: "Aleksandr Archipenko," 12; Andersen Galleries, 6, (illus. only); Archipenko, 1924, 34, (illus. only); Archipenko, 1960, pl. 72, (illus. only); "Archipenko at Kingore's," 8; Bohan, 57, 134; Brinton, (illus. only); "Brooklyn, City of Homes . . .," 9, (illus. only); *Buffalo Courier-Express*, 4, (illus. only); Bulliet, (illus. only); Dreier, 77, (illus. only); Hekking, 168, (illus. only); Herbert, Apter, and Kenney, 47-48, cat. 11 (illus.); Hildebrandt, 15, fig. 64, (illus.); "It's Modern Whether Coming or Going," 15, (illus.); Karshan, April, 1968, 37; Karshan 1969, 72, fig. 102, (illus. only); Karshan, 1975, 95, (illus.), 109; Licht, 334, (illus. only); Little Gallery, 13, (illus. only); Marter, 73-74, (illus.); McBride, 5; Michaelsen, ill. 24, (illus. only); Moholy-Nagy, (illus. only); Museum of Modern Art, 19, cat. 154, (illus.); "Palette and Brush;" "A Provocative Sculptor, Alexander Archipenko," 21, (illus.): Rich, 23; Seredynsky, 11, (illus. only); Teige, cat. 11, (illus. only); Wiese, 1923, pl. XXVII, (illus. only); Yale University Art Gallery, 23-24, (illus.).

I-5. **FIGURE,** 1917 (1930s?)
Painted wood relief
27 × 20½″
Collection of Frances Archipenko Gray, New York

Bibliography: Kramer, 1970, 17, (illus.); Lieberman and Kuh, cat. 21, cover, (illus. only); Michaelsen, 213, cat. S120, (illus.); Wight, 69, (illus. only).

I-6. **RELIEF,** 1936 (1950s?)
Aluminum
43¼ × 9¼″
Collection of Frances Archipenko Gray, New York

Bibliography: Pace Gallery, cat. 15, (illus. only); Wiese, 1960, cat. 36, (illus. only).

I-7. **VENUS,** 1953
Wood, mother of pearl mosaic
60″ high
Collection of Frances Archipenko Gray, New York

Bibliography: Archipenko, 1960, 46, 86, pl. 73, (illus.); Associated American Artists, 1954, cat. 40, cover, (illus. only); Karshan, 1975, 143, (illus. only); Rzepecki, June 1955, 12, (illus. only); Rzepecki, July 1955, 2, (illus. only); Syracuse Museum of Fine Arts, 21, cat. 73, (illus. only); Wiese, 1955, cat. 42 (illus. only); Wiese, 1960, cat. 45, (illus. only).

I-8. **REVOLVING FIGURE,** 1956
Wood, mother of pearl mosaic, formica, metal
78″ high
Collection of Frances Archipenko Gray, New York

Bibliography: Archipenko, 1960, 60, pl. 189-192, (illus. four views); Karshan, April, 1967, 14; Masheck, 79; Perls Galleries, 1957, cat. 6, (illus. only); G.S., 16.

I-9. **MULTI-COLORED FIGURE,** 1957
Wood, metal, bakelite
52×26″
Collection of Frances Archipenko Gray, New York

Bibliography: Galleria San Fedele, cat. 44, fig. 4, (illus. only); Sangiorgi and Recupero, cat. 44, pl. 19, (illus. only); Wiese, 1960, cat. 52, (illus. only); Wight, Kuh, and Karshan, 26-7, 54, cat. 52, (illus.).

I-10. **BALLERINA,** 1957
Wood and metal
27×14″
Collection of Frances Archipenko Gray, New York

II. RECLINING FIGURES

II-1. **TORSO IN SPACE,** 1936
Bronze 6/6
60″ long
Collection of Frances Archipenko Gray, New York

Bibliography: Archipenko, 1960, pl. 184, (illus. only); "Archipenko Bronzes," 9, (illus. only); Atirnomis, 59; Brazu (illus. only); Goodrich and Baur, 66, (illus. only); Karshan, April, 1968, 38; Karshan, 1968, 52, cat. 22, (illus. only); Karshan, 1969, 78, cat. 52, fig. 114, (illus. only); McCabe, 236, 238, pl. 93, (illus.); Palais des Beaux-Arts de Bruxelles, 26, cat. 52, (illus. only); Perls Galleries, 1959, cat. 22, cover, (illus. only); Robbins, 147, pl. 217, (illus. only); Schnell, 128, fig. 182, (illus.); Tarbell, 40, pl. 52, (illus.); Wasserman, 63, note 1; Wight, Kuh, and Karshan, 25.

II-2. **TORSO IN SPACE,** 1952
Lithography, serigraphy, embossing
24¾×14⅞″
Edition of 50
Collection of Frances Archipenko Gray, New York

Bibliography: Campbell, 98; Karshan, 1967, 74, (illus.); Karshan, 1968, 31, 34, pl. 29, (illus.), 61, cat. 49, (illus.); Karshan, 1975, 125, cat. 37, (illus.); Wight, Kuh, and Karshan, 32, 33, cat. 107, (illus.).

II-3. **COLLAGE (TORSO),** 1953
Collage with perforated surface, wood, paper
18×24″
Collection of Frances Archipenko Gray, New York

Bibliography: Archipenko, 1960, pl. 273, (illus. only); Karshan, 1968, 31, 32, pl. 26, (illus.); Karshan, 1975, 125, (illus.); Pace Gallery, cover, (illus. only); Wiese, 1955, cat. 52, (illus. only).

II-4. **COLLAGE (TORSO),** 1954
Collage with perforated surface, wood, metal
18×28″
Collection of Frances Archipenko Gray, New York

Bibliography: Archipenko, 1960, pl. 272, (illus. only); Karshan, 1968, 31, 33, pl. 27, (illus.), 53, cat. 25, (illus.); Karshan, 1975, 125; McCabe, 239, pl. 94, (illus. only); Wasserman, 10, (illus.), 66, cat. 51, (illus.).

II-5. **CLEOPATRA (REPOSE),** 1957
Wood, bakelite, polychrome
38×84″
Collection of Frances Archipenko Gray, New York

Bibliography: Archipenko, 1960, pl. 7, (illus. only); Karshan, April, 1967, 14; Karshan, April 1968, 38; Karshan, 1968, 30, (illus.), 31, 34; Karshan, 1975, 125, (illus.); Masheck, 79; Perls Galleries, 1957, cat. 21, (illus. only); Sangiorgi, 37,(illus. only); Wasserman, 66; Wiese, 1960, cat. 51, (illus. only); Wight, Kuh, and Karshan, 26, (illus.), 27-28.

II-6. **FIGURE,** 1960
Colored pencil and tempera
28×22″
Collection of Frances Archipenko Gray, New York

II-7. **FIGURE,** 1960
Colored pencil and tempera
27×21″
Collection of Frances Archipenko Gray, New York

II-8. **RECLINING FIGURE (REPOSE),** 1960
Watercolor and ink
8½ × 11″
Collection of Frances Archipenko Gray, New York

II-9. **RECLINING FIGURE,** 1950s
Pencil
15 × 22″
Collection of Frances Archipenko Gray, New York

II-10. **RECLINING FIGURE,** 1950s
Pencil
15 × 22″
Collection of Frances Archipenko Gray, New York

III. STILL LIFE

III-1. **STILL LIFE WITH VASE,** 1921
Lithograph
17⅛ × 9½″
Edition of 60
From the portfolio *Alexandre Archipenko: Dreizehn Steinzeichnungen,*
Verlag Ernst Wasmuth, Berlin

Bibliography: Karshan, 1968, 59, cat. 43, pl. 21, (illus. only); Karshan, 1975, 85, cat. 10, (illus.); Herbert, Apter, and Kenney, 46, cat. 10K.

III-2. **STILL LIFE,** 1950s
Brush and ink
18½ × 12¼″
Collection of Frances Archipenko Gray, New York

III-3. **OBJECTS ON THE TABLE,** 1957
Painted wood relief
25 × 17″
Collection of Frances Archipenko Gray, New York

Bibliography: Archipenko, 1960, pl. 9, (illus. only); Fabbri, pl. XVI, (illus.); Perls Galleries, 1957, cat. 23, (illus. only); Wight, Kuh, and Karshan, 55, cat. 56, (illus. only).

III-4. **OBJECTS ON THE TABLE,** 1957
Bronze
25 × 17″
Collection of Frances Archipenko Gray, New York

Bibliography: Wight, Kuh, and Karshan, 67, cat. 57.

III-5. **STILL LIFE WITH BOOK AND VASE ON TABLE,** 1960 (1918)
Bronze
18 × 13¾″
Collection of Frances Archipenko Gray, New York

Bibliography: Bremer Skulpturenausstellung, (illus. only); Coates, 73; Eckhardt, 10, cat. 17, (illus. only); Galerie Stangl, fig. 24, (illus. only); Hofmann, 21, cat. 17, (illus. only); Karshan, 1968, 27, 28, pl. 20, (illus.), 50, cat. 17, (illus.); Karshan, 1969, 44, cat. 34, (illus. only); Karshan, 1975, 85, (illus.); Michaelsen, ill. 22, (illus.); Perls Galleries, 1962, cat. 9, (illus. only); Sangiorgi, 37, (illus. only); Sangiorgi and Recupero, cat. 24, cover, (illus. only); Taillander, (illus. only); Wight, Kuh, and Karshan, 20, cat. 34, (illus.), 23.

IV. GROUP FIGURES AND FRAGMENTARY FIGURES

IV-1. **REVELATION,** 1952
Ink, gouache, gold leaf on canvas
36 × 18″
Collection of Frances Archipenko Gray, New York

Bibliography: Karshan, 1968, 38, fig. 34, (illus.), 58, cat. 40, (illus.); Karshan, 1969, 97, fig. 151, (illus. only); Pace Gallery, cat. 32; Pfeiffer, cover, (illus. only).

IV-2. **TWO FIGURES,** 1952
Serigraph
26¼ × 16″
Edition of 50
Collection of Frances Archipenko Gray, New York

Bibliography: Karshan, 1975, 121, cat. 35, (illus.);Ukrainian Art Exhibit Committee, cat. 11, (illus. only).

IV-3. **TWO FIGURES (MEDIEVAL),** 1954
Gouache
33 × 27″
Collection of Frances Archipenko Gray, New York

IV-4. **ORANGE AND BLACK,** 1957
Wood, metal, bakelite
25 × 48″
Collection of Frances Archipenko Gray, New York

Bibliography: Archipenko, 1960, pl. 11, (illus. only); Karshan, 1975, 143, (illus.); Perls Galleries, 1957, cat. 22, (illus. only); Sangiorgi and Recupero, cat. 46, pl. 20, (illus. only); Wiese, 1960, cat. 53, (illus. only); Wight, Kuh, and Karshan, 53, cat. 53, (illus. only).

IV-5. **RED,** 1957
Wood, bakelite
48 × 36″
Collection of Frances Archipenko Gray, New York

Bibliography: Archipenko, 1960, pl. 8, (illus. only); Brazu, cover, (illus. only); Wasserman, 66.

IV-6. **OVAL FIGURE,** 1957
Wood, metal, bakelite
43 × 36½″
Collection of Frances Archipenko Gray, New York

Bibliography: Archipenko, 1960, pl. 54, (illus. only); Bernard Danenberg Galleries, 4, 5, cat. 22, (illus.); Fabbri, pl. XVII, cover, (illus.); Karshan, 1975, 153, (illus.); Perls Galleries, 1957, cat. 19, (illus. only); Wight, Kuh, and Karshan, 27, 53, cat. 50, (illus.).

IV-7. **WHITE,** 1957
Wood, bakelite
37 × 43″
Collection of Frances Archipenko Gray, New York

Bibliography: Archipenko, 1960, pl. 25, (illus. only); Perls Galleries, 1957, cat. 26, (illus. only); Wasserman, 66-7, cat. 52, (illus.).

IV-8. **CONVERSATION,** 1959
Bronze on marble 1/6
27 × 14½″
Collection of Frances Archipenko Gray, New York

Bibliography: "Archipenko Bronzes," 9, fig. 5, (illus. only); Brazu, fig. 5, (illus. only); Galerie Stangl, fig. 43, (illus. only); Karshan, 1975, 133, (illus. only); Perls Galleries, 1959, cat. 34, (illus. only); Wiese, 1960, cat. 67, (illus. only).

IV-9. **TWO FIGURES,** 1959
Bronze on marble 59-1
21 × 14½″
Collection of Frances Archipenko Gray, New York

IV-10. **FRAGMENTARY RELIEF,** 1959
Bronze on marble 1/6
23 × 14″
Collection of Frances Archipenko Gray, New York

Bibliography: Archipenko, 1960, pl. 134, (illus. only); Galerie Stangl, fig. 41, (illus. only); Hofmann, 29, (illus. only); Sangiorgi and Recupero, 21, cat. 46, (illus. only); Wiese, 1960, cat. 65, (illus.); Wight, Kuh, and Karshan, 24, cat. 61, (illus. only).

IV-11. **EAGLE,** 1959
Bronze on marble 1/8
10½ × 15½″
Collection of Frances Archipenko Gray, New York

Bibliography: Karshan, 1975, 141, (illus.); A.J.M., 15, (illus.); Munsterberg, 55, Wight, Kuh, and Karshan, 12, cat. 59, (illus. only).

IV-12. **WOMAN WITH FAN,** c.1958 (1914)
Bronze
35″ high
Collection of Frances Archipenko Gray, New York

Bibliography: Coates, 73; Cooper, 243, pl. 292, (illus.); Dorival, 211, fig. 55, (illus.), 212; Eckhardt, 6, cat. 13, (illus. only); Galerie Stangl, fig. 15, (illus. only); Galleria San Fedele, cat. 15, (illus. only); Hofmann, 32, cat. 8, (illus. only); Karshan, April, 1968, 36, (illus. only); Karshan, 1968, 11, cat. 15, (illus. only); Karshan 1969, 43, cat. 22, (illus. only); Karshan, 1974, 17, fig. 19, (illus.); Michaelsen, ill. 25, (illus.); "New Day for Old Cubist," 79, (illus. only); "Notable Works of Art Now on the Market," pl. LXXIX, (illus. only); Perls Galleries, 1962, cat. 6, (illus. only); Read, 73, pl. 70, (illus. only); Sangiorgi and Recupero, cat. 15, cover, (illus. only); Taillander, (illus. only); Wight, Kuh, and Karshan, 17, cat. 23, (illus.).

IV-13. **STANDING WOMAN,** c.1960 (1920)
Bronze 3/8
28½ × 16⅜″
Collection of Frances Archipenko Gray, New York

Bibliography: Galerie Stangl, fig. 26, (illus. only); Hofmann, 36, cat. 19, (illus. only); Michaelsen, ill. 23, (illus.); Perls Galleries, 1962, cat. 10, (illus. only); Sangiorgi, 37, (illus. only); Sangiorgi and Recupero, 16, cat. 26, (illus. only); Wight, Kuh, and Karshan, 21, cat. 36, (illus.).

IV-14. **TWO FIGURES,** 1960
Gouache and colored pencil
21½ × 27½″
Collection of Frances Archipenko Gray, New York

Bibliography: Wight, Kuh, and Karshan, 60, cat. 89, (illus. only).

IV-15. **TWO FIGURES,** 1961
Gouache, colored pencil, pastel
28⅖ × 22⅖″
Collection of Frances Archipenko Gray, New York

IV-16. **PROPHET AND WOMAN,** 1961
Gouache, pastel
26½ × 21¼″
Collection of Frances Archipenko Gray, New York

Bibliography: Karshan, 1975, 131, (illus.); Sangiorgi, 41, (illus. only).

IV-17. **HERODIAS AND SALOME,** 1962
Lithograph
25¼ × 19¼″
Edition of 20
Collection of Frances Archipenko Gray, New York

Bibliography: Karshan, 1975, 131, cat. 40, (illus.); Karshan, n.d., 24, pl. 173, (illus.).

IV-18. **TWO FIGURES,** 1961
Gouache, colored pencil
28⅖ × 22⅖″
Collection of Frances Archipenko Gray, New York

IV-19. **THREE FIGURES,** 1962
Gouache
12 × 14½″
Collection of Frances Archipenko Gray, New York

Bibliography: Sangiorgi, 40, (illus. only).

IV-20. **THREE FRAGMENTARY FIGURES (FLUCTUATING FIGURES),** 1962
Collage, chalk
28½ × 22″
Collection of Frances Archipenko Gray, New York

Bibliography: Fuchs, cat. 70, (illus. only); Hofmann, 36, pl. 9, (illus. only); Pace Gallery, cat. 43; Sangiorgi and Recupero, cat. 114, pl. 27, (illus. only).

IV-21. **SEATED AND STANDING FIGURES,** 1962
Lithograph
23¼ x 17¼"
Collection of Frances Archipenko Gray, New York

Bibliography: Karshan, 1975, 129, cat. 39, (illus.).

IV-22. **ENCOUNTER,** 1963
Lithograph
19¾ x 10⅞"
Edition of 50
Collection of Frances Archipenko Gray, New York

Bibliography: Karshan, 1975, 133, cat. 42, (illus.).

IV-23. **LIVING FORMS (LES FORMES VIVANTES),** 1962-1963
Lithographs
Editions of 75
From the portfolio *Les formes vivantes,* Erker-Presse, St. Gallen, Switzerland, 1963

Bibliography: Karshan, April, 1967, 14; Karshan, 1969, 113; Karshan, 1975, 57-59; Kramer, 1967, 23; Musée des Beaux-Arts de Lyon, cat.s 95-104; C.R., 44; Wight, Kuh, and Karshan, 34.

IV-23.1. **THE LOVERS**
22¾ x 14¾"

Bibliography: Karshan, 1968, 61, cat. 51, (illus. only); Karshan, 1975, 137, cat. 44, (illus.).

IV-23.2. **BLACK DANCE**
21½ x 10¼"

Bibliography: Hofmann, 23, (illus. only); Karshan, 1968, 62, cat. 52, (illus. only); Karshan, 1975, 139, cat. 45, (illus.).

IV-23.3. **THE GROUP**
26 x 17½"

Bibliography: Karshan, 1968, 62, cat. 53, (illus. only); Karshan, 1969, frontispiece, (illus. only); Karshan, 1975, 141, cat. 46 (illus.).

IV-23.4a. **THE MANNIKINS**
25½ x 15¾"

Bibliography: Karshan, 1968, 62, cat. 54, (illus. only); Karshan, 1975, 143, cat. 47, (illus.).

IV-23.4b. **THE MANNIKINS**
Drawing for the lithograph *The Mannikins*
Ink, pencil, crayon
Collection of Frances Archipenko Gray, New York

IV-23.5. **THE FAMILY OF ONE FORM**
26¼ x 18"

Bibliography: Karshan, 1968, 63, cat. 55, (illus. only); Karshan, 1975, 144, cat. 48, (illus.).

IV-23.6. **CORONATION OF FORMS**
25 x 17½"

Bibliography: Karshan, 1968, 63, cat. 56, (illus. only); Karshan, 1975, 145, cat. 49, (illus.); Wight, Kuh, and Kárshan, 62, cat. 114, (illus. only).

IV-23.7a. **ENCIRCLED FORMS**
17×27½″

Bibliography: Karshan, 1968, 63, cat. 57, (illus. only); Karshan, 1975, 147, cat. 50, (illus.); Wight, 69, (illus. only); Wight, Kuh, and Karshan, 32.

IV-23.8. **THE LUMINOSITY OF FORMS**
26½ × 17½″

Bibliography: Karshan, 1967, 76, (illus. only); Karshan, 1968, 22, pl. 14, (illus.), 17, 64, cat. 58, (illus.); Karshan, 1969, 104, cat. 102, fig. 171, (illus. only); Karshan, 1975, 149, cat. 51, (illus.); Wight, Kuh, and Karshan, 31, cat. 116, (illus. only).

IV-23.9a. **MAJESTIC FORMS**
25¾ × 18⅝″

Bibliography: "Archipenko Retrospective at Kovler Gallery," 29, (illus. only); Binoche, 51, (illus.); Musée des Beaux-Arts de Lyon, cat. 103, fig. 16, (illus. only); Karshan, 1967, 75, (illus. only); Karshan, 1968, 23, 26, pl. 19, (illus.), 64, cat. 59, (illus.); Karshan, 1975, 151, cat. 52, (illus.); Wight, Kuh, and Karshan, 63, cat. 117, (illus. only).

IV-23.9b. **FIGURE WITH ORANGE BACKGROUND**
(Drawing for the lithograph *Majestic Forms)*
Gouche, chalk
31¾ × 26¼″
Collection of Frances Archipenko Gray, New York

IV-23.10. **RENDEZVOUS OF FOUR FORMS**
25½ × 20⅛″

Bibliography: Karshan, 1968, 64, cat. 60, (illus. only); Karshan, 1975, 153, cat. 53, (illus.); Wight, Kuh, and Karshan, 64, cat. 118, (illus. only).

V. OTHER WORKS

V-1. **THE MOON,** 1947
Carved plastic, electric light
12 × 12½″
Collection of Frances Archipenko Gray, New York

Bibliography: Archipenko, 1960, 60, pl. 199, (illus.).

BIBLIOGRAPHY TO THE CATALOGUE

by Nicholas J. Capasso

"Aleksandr Archipenko," *The New York Times*, January 27, 1924, section 7, 12.

Anderson Galleries, *Archipenko: Catalogue of Exhibition and Description of Archipentura*, exhibition catalogue, New York, 1928.

Archipenko, Alexander, "Nature the Point of Departure," *The Arts*, 5, January, 1924, 32-36.

———, *Archipenko: Fifty Creative Years*, TEKHNE, New York, 1960.

"Archipenko at Kingore's," *Art News*, January 26, 1924, 8.

"Archipenko Bronzes," *Ameryka*, 62, 8-9.

"Archipenko Retrospective at Kovler Gallery, *Art Scene*, 2, November, 1968, 29.

Associated American Artists, *40 Years of Inventive Sculpture by Archipenko*, exhibition catalogue, Associated American Artists New York Galleries, New York, 1948.

———, *Archipenko, 110th Exhibition: Fifty Years Production*, exhibition catalogue, Associated American Artists Galleries, New York, 1954.

Atirnomis, "Archipenko at MOMA and Danenberg," *Arts Magazine*, 45, September-October, 1970, 59.

Barr, Alfred H., *Cubism and Abstract Art*, exhibition catalogue, Museum of Modern Art, New York, 1936.

Bernard Danenberg Galleries, *Archipenko: The American Years, 1923-1963*, exhibition catalogue, New York, 1970.

Binoche, M., *Gravures, multiples d'aujourd'hui sculpture sélénite*, exhibition catalogue, Hôtel Drouot, Paris, 1972; 51 (illus. only).

Bohan, Ruth L., *The Société Anonyme's Brooklyn Exhibition: Katherine Dreier and Modernism in America*, UMI Research Press, Ann Arbor, 1982.

Bowdoin College Museum of Fine Arts, *Colored Drawings by Alexander Archipenko*, exhibition catalogue, Brunswick, Maine, 1950.

Brazu, Rzeźby Z., "Archipenko," *Ameryka* 31.

Bremer Skulpturenausstellung 4, *Skulptur und Farbe*, exhibition catalogue, Bremen, 1983.

Brinton, Christian, *The Archipenko Exhibition*, exhibition catalogue, Kingore Gallery, New York, 1924.

"Brooklyn, City of Homes, Has Another Revel in Abstract Art," *Art Digest*, 1, December 1, 1926, 9.

Buffalo Courier-Express, March 6, 1927, Rotogravure Section, 4.

Bulliett, C.J., *Tour of the Exhibition of the Works of Alexander Archipenko*, Chicago, 1927.

Campbell, Lawrence, "Reviews and Previews: Alexander Archipenko," *Art News*, 72, November, 1973, 98.

Casson, Stanley, *Twentieth Century Sculptors*, Oxford University Press, London, 1930.

Coates, Robert M., "The Art Galleries: Sense of the Past," *The New Yorker*, 37, January 20, 1962, 70-74.

Cooper, Douglass, *The Cubist Epoch*, exhibition catalogue, Phaidon Press Ltd. in association with the Los Angeles Museum of Art and the Metropolitan Museum of Art, London, 1971.

Courthion, Pierre, "Le plus grand musée de sculpture du monde: La collection Hirshhorn," *XXe siècle*, 45, December, 1975, 28-35.

Däubler, Theodor, and Goll, Iwan, *Archipenko-Album*, Gustav Kiepenheuer Verlag, Potsdam, 1921.

Dorival, Bernard, "Les omissions d'Archipenko et de Lipchitz," *Bulletin de la Société de l'Histoire de l'Art Français*, 1974, 201-20.

Dreier, Katherine and Aladjalov, Constantin, *Modern Art*, Société Anonyme—Museum of Modern Art, New York, 1926, reprinted in *Selected Publications: Societe Anonyme (The First Museum of Modern Art: 1920-1944), Volume I: Documents*, Arno Series of Contemporary Art, Arno Press, New York, 1972.

Eckhardt, Ferdinand, *Alexander Archipenko Exhibition*, exhibition catalogue, Winnipeg Art Gallery, Winnipeg, 1962.

Elsen, Albert E., *Pioneers of Modern Sculpture*, exhibition catalogue, Hayward Gallery, London, 1973.

Fabbri, Dino, ed., "Archipenko," *I maestri della scultura 44*, Fratelli Fabbri Editori, Milan, 1966.

Fuchs, Heinz, *Alexander Archipenko: Zeichnungen, Aquarelle, 1912-1962*, exhibition catalogue, Kunsthalle Mannheim, Mannheim, 1962.

Galerie Stangl, *Archipenko '64*, exhibition catalogue, Munich, 1964.

Galleria San Fedele, *Mostra antologica di Archipenko*, exhibition catalogue, Milan, 1963.

Goll, Ivan, *Archipenko: An Appreciation*, Société Anonyme, Inc., New York, 1921, reprinted in *Selected Publications: Société Anonyme (The First Museum of Modern Art: 1920-1944), Volume II: Pamphlets*, Arno Series of Contemporary Art, Arno Press, New York, 1972.

Goodrich, Lloyd, and Baur, John I.H., *American Art of our Century*, Frederick A. Praeger, New York, 1961.

Hammacher, A.M., *The Evolution of Modern Sculpture: Tradition and Innovation,* Harry N. Abrams, Inc., New York, 1969.

Hekking, William M., "Moderns at the Albright Art Gallery," *Buffalo Arts Journal,* 9, March, 1927, 167-69.

Herbert, Robert L., Apter, Eleanor S., and Kenney, Elise K., *The Société Anonyme and the Dreier Bequest at Yale University: A Catalogue Raisonné,* Yale University Press, New Haven, 1984.

Hildebrandt, Hans, *Alexander Archipenko,* Ukrainske Slowo Publishers Ltd., Berlin, 1923.

Hofmann, Werner, *Alexander Archipenko,* exhibition catalogue, Galerie "Im Erker", St. Gallen, Switzerland, 1962.

"It's Modern Art Whether Coming or Going," *The New York Herald,* July 22, 1923, 15.

Janis, Harriet, and Blesh, Rudi, *Collage: Personalities, Concepts, Techniques,* Chilton Co., Philadelphia, 1962.

Karshan, Donald H., "Alexander Archipenko—In Retrospect," *Journal of the Archives of American Art,* 7, April, 1967, 4-15.

———, "The Graphics of Archipenko," *Artist's Proof,* 7, 1967, 72-77.

———, "Archipenko: A Rediscovered Modern Master on Tour," *Arts Magazine,* 42, April, 1968, 36-38.

———, *Archipenko: Content and Continuity 1908-1963,* exhibition catalogue, Kovler Gallery, Chicago, 1968.

———, ed., *Archipenko: International Visionary,* exhibition catalogue, National Collection of Fine Arts, Smithsonian Institution Press, Washington, D.C., 1969.

———, "Les revolutions d'Alexandre Archipenko," *Plaisir de France,* 40, July-August, 1974, 12-17.

———, *Archipenko: The Sculpture and Graphic Art, Including a Print Catalogue Raisonné,* Westview Press, Boulder, Colorado, 1975.

———, *The Emergent Graphics,* Graphics Editions, Solomon and Company Fine Art, New York, (n.d.).

Kramer, Hilton, "The Innovations of Archipenko," *The New York Times,* May 14, 1967, section D, 23.

———, "The Two Archipenkos," *The New York Times,* August 2, 1970, section 2, 17.

Lerner, Abraham, ed., *The Hirshhorn Museum and Sculpture Garden,* Harry N. Abrams Inc., New York, 1974.

Licht, Fred, Sculpture, *Nineteenth and Twentieth Centuries,* Greenwich, Connecticut, 1967.

Lieberman, William, and Kuh, Katherine, *Archipenko: The Parisian Years,* exhibition catalogue, Museum of Modern Art, New York, 1970.

Little Gallery, *Machine Age Exposition Catalogue,* exhibition catalogue, New York, 1927.

A.J.M., "Reviews and Previews: Archipenko," *Art News,* 58, October, 1959, 15.

Marter, Joan, "Constructivism in America: The 1930s," *Arts Magazine,* 56, June, 1982, 73-80.

Masheck, Joseph, "Reviews: Alexander Archipenko, Pace Gallery," *Artforum,* 12, December, 1973, 78-79.

McBride, Henry, "Brooklyn Museum Indulges in Most Modern of Art Displays Mirroring the Time: Machine-Made Age Presented with Disturbing Frankness," *New York Sun,* November 27, 1926, 5.

McCabe, Cynthia J., *The Golden Door: Artist-Immigrants of America, 1876-1976,* exhibition catalogue, Hirshhorn Museum and Sculpture Garden, Smithsonian Institution Press, Washington, D.C., 1976.

Michaelsen, Katherine J., *Archipenko: A Study of the Early Works, 1908-1920,* Garland Publishing Inc., New York, 1977.

Moholy-Nagy, Laszlo, *The New Vision,* trans. D. Hoffman, New York, 1938.

Munsterberg, Hugo, "In the Galleries: Archipenko," *Arts Magazine,* 34, October, 1959, 55.

Musee des Beaux-Arts de Lyon, *Alexandre Archipenko,* exhibition catalogue, Lyon, 1969.

Museum of Modern Art, *Modern Works of Art: Fifth Anniversary Exhibition,* exhibition catalogue, New York, 1934.

"New Day for Old Cubist," *Life—International Edition,* March 26, 1962, 78-80.

"Notable Works of Art Now on the Market," *Burlington Magazine,* 110, supplement, 1968, 12.

Pace Gallery, *Archipenko at Pace,* exhibition catalogue, Pace Editions Inc., New York, 1973.

Palais des Beaux-Arts de Bruxelles, *Archipenko,* exhibition catalogue, Brussels, 1969.

"Palette and Brush," *Town Topics,* January 31, 1924.

Perls Galleries, *Archipenko (1887-) Recent Polychromes,* exhibition catalogue, New York, 1957.

———, *Alexander Archipenko (1887-) Bronzes,* exhibition catalogue, New York, 1959.

———, *Alexander Archipenko (1887-) Bronzes,* exhibition catalogue, New York, 1962.

Pfeiffer, Wolfgang, *Desenhos de Archipenko,* exhibition catalogue, Museo de Arte Moderna de São Paolo, 1952.

Philadelphia Museum of Art, *The Louise and Walter Arensberg Collection: Twentieth Century Section,* Philadelphia, 1954.

"A Provocative Sculptor: Alexander Archipenko," *Shadowland,* 8, July, 1923, 21.

C.R., "In the Museums: Alexander Archipenko," *Arts Magazine,* 40, December, 1965, 44.

Ratcliff, Carter, "Domesticated Nightmares," *Art in America,* 73, May, 1975, 145-51.

Raynal, Maurice, *Archipenko avec 32 reproductions en phototypie,* Editions de "Valori Plastici," Rome, 1923.

Read, Herbert, *A Concise History of Modern Sculpture,* Frederick A. Praeger, Publishers, New York, 1966.

Rich, Catherine J., "Four Children and the Moderns," *Brooklyn Museum Quarterly,* 14, January, 1927, 23.

Robbins, Daniel, "Statues to Sculpture: From the Nineties to the Thirties," in *Two Hundred Years of American Sculpture,* exhibition catalogue, Whitney Museum of American Art, New York, 1976.

Roberts, Kieth, "Acquisitions of Modern Art by Museums: Washington, D.C., Hirshhorn Museum and Sculpture Garden," *Burlington Magazine,* 116, November 1974, 702.

Rowell, Margit, *The Planar Dimension: Europe, 1912-1932,* exhibition catalogue, Solomon Guggenheim Museum, New York, 1979.

Rzepecki, Nestor, "An Exclusive Interview with One of the Top Names in World Art," *Pace,* June, 1955, 11-17.

———, "Archipenko," *Nowi Dni, A Ukrainian Monthly,* 6, July, 1955, 1-4.

G.S., "Alexander Archipenko," *Pictures on Exhibit,* October, 1957, 16-18.

Salon d'Automne, *Grandes oeuvres russes des collections françaises,* exhibition catalogue, Grand Palais, Paris, 1972.

Sangiorgi, Giovanni, "La pittura scultorea di Archipenko," *Civilità delle macchine,* September-October, 1963, 35-42.

Sangiorgi, Giovanni, and Recupero, Jacopo, *Alexander Archipenko,* exhibition catalogue, Edizioni dell'Ente Premi, Rome, 1963.

Schnell, Werner, *Der Torso als Problem der Modernen Kunst,* Gebr. Mann Verlag, Berlin, 1980.

Seredynsky, Edward, "Alexander Archipenko," *The Trident,* 5, January-February, 1941, 6-14.

Stein, Donna, "Cubism in Prints," *Print Review,* 18, 1983, 37-53.

Syracuse Museum of Fine Arts, *One Hundred and Twenty-five Years of American Art,* exhibition catalogue, Syracuse, New York, 1953.

Taillandier, Yvon, "Conversation avec Archipenko," *XXe siècle,* 22, December, 1963, supplement.

Taggard, M., "Picasso's "Woman with a Fan" as an Icon," *The Nelson Gallery and Atkins Museum Bulletin,* 5, no. 7, 1982, 83-87.

Tarbell, Roberta K., "Figurative Interpretations of Vanguard Concepts", in Marter, Joan, Tarbell, Roberta K., and Wechsler, Jeffrey, *Vanguard American Sculpture 1913-1939,* exhibition catalogue, Rutgers University Art Gallery, New Brunswick, New Jersey, 1979, 29-44.

Teige, K., *Archipenko,* exhibition catalogue, Publikace Devĕtsilu, Prague, 1923.

Ukrainian Art Exhibit Committee, *Ukrainian Art Exhibit,* exhibition catalogue, McGregor Memorial Community Arts Center, Wayne State University, Detroit, 1960.

Wasserman, Jeanne L., *Three American Sculptors and the Female Nude: Lachaise, Nadelman, Archipenko,* exhibition catalogue, Fogg Art Museum, Harvard University, Cambridge, 1980.

Wiese, Erich, *Alexander Archipenko,* Junge Kunst Band 40, Verlag von Klinkhardt und Biermann, Leipzig, 1923.

———, *Alexander Archipenko: Plastik, Malerei, Zeichnungen, Druckgraphik,* exhibition catalogue, Hessisches Landesmuseum, Darmstadt, 1955.

———, *Archipenko: Plastiken 1909-1959,* exhibition catalogue, Kunstmuseum Düsseldorf, Düsseldorf, 1960.

Wight, Frederick S., "Retrospective for Archipenko," *Art in America,* 55, May-June, 1967, 64-69.

Wight, Frederick S., Kuh, Katherine, and Karshan, Donald, *Alexander Archipenko: A Memorial Exhibition,* exhibition catalogue, University of California, Los Angeles, Art Galleries, Los Angeles, 1967.

Yale University Art Gallery, *Collection of the Société Anonyme: Museum of Modern Art 1920,* Case, Lockwood, and Brainard, New Haven, 1950.